Poetry of Place

Poetry of Place

Helping Students Write Their Worlds

Terry Hermsen
Otterbein College, Westerville, Ohio

National Council of Teachers of English
1111 W. Kenyon Road, Urbana, Illinois 61801-1096

Staff Editor: Carol Roehm-Stogsdill

Interior Design: Doug Burnett

Cover Design: Frank Cucciarre, Blink Concept & Design, Inc.

Top Cover Image: A collage of iStockphoto.com images. iStockphoto.com/ Nicholas Monu, iStockphoto.com/Luis Bellagamba, iStockphoto.com/Peter Zelei, and iStockphoto.com/Phil Morley.

Bottom Cover Images: Photographed by Frank Cucciarre at Perrysburg (OH) Junior High School.

NCTE Stock Number: 36089

It is the policy of NCTE in its journals and other publications to provide a forum for the open discussion of ideas concerning the content and the teaching of English and the language arts. Publicity accorded to any particular point of view does not imply endorsement by the Executive Committee, the Board of Directors, or the membership at large, except in announcements of policy, where such endorsement is clearly specified.

Every effort has been made to provide URLs that were accurate when the text was written, but because of the rapidly changing nature of the Web, some sites and addresses may no longer be accessible.

Library of Congress Cataloging-in-Publication Data

Hermsen, Terry, 1950–
    Poetry of place : helping students write their worlds / Terry Hermsen.
        p. cm.
    "NCTE Stock Number: 36089."
    Includes bibliographical references and index.
    ISBN 978-0-8141-3608-9 (pbk.)
    1. Poetry—Study and teaching. I. Title.
    PN1101.H44 2009
    808.1—dc22

                                                                2008045886

This book is dedicated to Jill Grubb and her students at Mt. Gilead High School for welcoming me into their midst; to Stuart Lishan, collaborator and friend, with whom many of these lessons were developed and refined; and to Sydney Walker, who helped shape the theories that guided me back into the poems.

The arts are neglected because they are based in perception, and perception is disdained because it is not assumed to involve thought. In fact, educators and administrators cannot justify giving the arts an important position in the curriculum unless they understand that the arts are the most powerful means of strengthening the perceptual component without which productive thinking is impossible in any field of endeavor.

—Rudolph Arnheim, *Visual Thinking*

We still ask [students] to think . . . but we seldom tell them what thinking means. We seldom tell them that it's just putting this and that together, it's just saying one thing in terms of another.

—Robert Frost, "Education by Poetry"

*Oh swallows, swallows, poems are not
The point. Finding again the world,
That is the point.*

—Howard Nemerov, "The Blue Swallows"

Contents

II The Mt. Gilead Project: A Semester with Poetry

Permission Acknowledgments

Grateful acknowledgment is made to the following for permission to reprint copyrighted material:

Images

Bellows, George (American, 1882–1925). *Polo at Lakewood*. 1910.
Oil on canvas.
Columbus Art Association Purchase. (1911.001)
Columbus Museum of Art, Ohio. (Figure 9.6)

Bruegel, Pieter the Elder. *Elck or Everyman*. 1558.
Drawing, $8^1/_2 \times 11^3/_4$ inches.
Courtesy of the Trustees of the British Museum, London. (Figure 3.1)

The Chevron and *The Frying Pan* from *The Moon Seen as a Slice of Pineapple* by Conrad Hilberry. Reprinted by permission of The University of Georgia Press. (Figure 3.5)

Klee, Paul (1879–1940). *Die Beschwingten (The Elated)*. 1930.
Pen and India ink on drawing paper mounted on board.
$11^1/_4 \times 8^3/_4$ inches.
Klee cat. no. 1930, Q3, 73. (Figure 3.6)

Klimt, Gustav. *Baby (Cradle)*. 1917/1918.
Oil on canvas, $43^5/_8 \times 43^1/_2$ inches.
Gift of Otto and Franciska Kallir with the help of Carol and Edwin Gaines Fullinwider Fund.
Image courtesy of the Board of Trustees, National Gallery of Art, Washington, D.C. (Figure 3.4)

Magritte, René (1898–1967) © ARS, NY. *La Méditation* (The Meditation). 1936.
Oil on canvas, 50 × 65 cm.
Private collection.
Photo credit: Banque d'Images, ADAGP/Art Resource, NY (Figure 9.4)

Magritte, René (1898–1967) © ARS, NY. *Les Belles Relations (The Beautiful Relations)*. 1967.
Oil on canvas, 41 × 33 cm.
Private collection.
Photo credit: Banque d'Images, ADAGP/Art Resource, NY (Figure 4.1)

Magritte, René (1898–1967) © ARS, NY. *Le Domaine d'Arnheim (The Domain of Arnheim)*, 1962.
Oil on canvas, 146 × 114 cm.
Musees Royaux des Beaux-Arts, Brussels, Belgium.
Photo credit: Banque d'Images, ADAGP/Art Resource, NY (Figure 1.1)

Magritte, René (1898–1967) © ARS, NY. *La Voix du Sang (The Voice of the Blood)*, 1948.
Private collection.
Photo credit: Herscovici/Art Resource, NY (Figure 9.1)

From the James Miller Collection of the Morrow County (Ohio) Historical Society:
Unknown photographer, "Philips and Son" (Figure 8.1)
Unknown photographer, "The Globe Hotel" (Figure 8.2)
Unknown photographer, "Snowy Street" (Figure 8.3)
Unknown photographer, "Casey Bending Garage" (Figure 8.4)
Unknown photographer, "Sister Vanatta" (Figure 8.5)
Unknown photographer, "Car Lift" (Figure 8.6)

O'Keeffe, Georgia (American, 1887–1986). *Autumn Leaves–Lake George, N.Y.* 1924.
Oil on canvas.
Museum Purchase, Howard Fund II. (1981.006)
Columbus Museum of Art, Ohio. (Figure 9.5)

Van Gogh, Vincent (1853–1890). *The Starry Night.* 1889.
Oil on canvas, 29 × 36 1/4 inches.
Acquired through the Lillie P. Bliss Bequest. (472.1941)
The Museum of Modern Art, New York, NY, U.S.A.
Digital Image © The Museum of Modern Art/Licensed by SCALA/Art Resource, NY (Figure 9.2)

Van Honthorst, Gerrit (Dutch, 1590–1656). *Samson and Delilah.* 1621.
Oil on canvas, 129 cm × 94 cm.
Acquisition: Mr. and Mrs. William H. Marlatt Fund. (1968.23)
Courtesy of © The Cleveland Museum of Art. (Figure 3.2)

Uelsmann, Jerry N. "Untitled photograph (man on desk)." 1976.
Used with the permission from Jerry Uelsmann, Inc. (Figure 9.3)

Other photographs were taken by Terry Hermsen, teacher Jill Grubb, and various students.

Poetry

"Kitchen Talk" from YEARS THAT ANSWER by Maggie Anderson. Published by Harper and Row Publishers, 1980. Used by permission of the author.

"Bantu Combinations" first appeared in THE LIFE OF A SOUTH AFRICAN TRIBE by Henri Junod. First published by Macmillan & Company, Ltd., 1912, and reprinted by Kessinger Publishing, 2003. "Bantu Combinations" was included in TECHNICIANS OF THE SACRED, edited by Jerome Rothenberg, published by Doubleday, 1969. Reprinted by permission of Kessinger Publishing.

"Surrealist Dialogues" from OUEVRE, VOL. 1 by Achille Chavée, translated by Nicole Ball. First appeared in TEACHERS & WRITERS COLLABORATIVE newsletter, January–February 1988.

"Pole Vaulter" by David Allen Evans. Reprinted by permission of the author.

"Chainsaw Inquiries" from INQUIRIES by Jeff Gundy. Copyright © 1992. Reprinted by permission of Bottom Dog Press.

"Bagworms in Their Tent above the River" and "Mr. Double-Eyes" from THE RIVER'S DAUGHTER by Terry Hermsen. Copyright © 2008. Reprinted by permission of Bottom Dog Press.

"The Chevron" and "The Frying Pan" from THE MOON SEEN AS A SLICE OF PINEAPPLE by Conrad Hilberry. Copyright © 1984. Used by permission of The University of Georgia Press.

"The Pencil's Dream" by Tymoteusz Karpowicz, from POSTWAR POLISH POETRY by Czeslaw Milosz, translation copyright © 1965 by Czeslaw Milosz. Used by permission of Doubleday, a division of Random House, Inc.

"One A.M." from COLLECTED EARLIER POEMS 1940–1960. Copyright © 1958 by Denise Levertov. Reprinted by permission of New Directions Publishing Corp.

"Childhood" from WATCH FIRE by Christopher Merrill. Copyright © 1994. Reprinted by permission of White Pine Press.

"The Word" from "Lost in the City" from MEMOIRS by Pablo Neruda, English translation by Hardie St. Martin. Copyright © 1974 by the Estate of Pablo Neruda. Translation copyright © 1977 by Farrar, Straus, and Giroux, LLC. Reprinted by permission of the publisher.

"Snakes in Winter" from TWELVE MOONS by Mary Oliver. Copyright ©1972, 1973, 1974, 1976, 1977, 1978, and 1979 by Mary Oliver. Reprinted by permission of Little, Brown & Company.

"The Builders" from CONCERNING THE BOOK THAT IS THE BODY OF THE BELOVED by Gregory Orr. Copyright © 2005 by Gregory Orr. Reprinted with the permission of Copper Canyon Press, www.coppercanyonpress.org.

Acknowledgments

Thank you:

- to the many other friends and teachers whose work, dedication to their students, and persistent ingenuity has inspired me over the years: Jann Gallagher, Leah Buturain, Colleen Webster, Amira Jarmakani, Mary Ann Titus, Cindy Fidler, Mitch Hoops, Joe Hecker, Jerri Seckel, Mary Hardgrove, Jan Redmond, Max Griffith, Dianne Avers, Mindy Holmes, Lani Meyers, Emilie Christof, Nancy Shew, Marky Schmidt, Brandy Wright, Emily Funston, Trina Marshall, and Paul McClintock, and so many others too numerous to name, in so many communities around Ohio.

- to my teachers and collaborators within the arts: poets Debbie Athy, David Hassler, Jeff Gundy, Christopher Merrill, Mimi Chenfeld, and Dionne Custer; fiction writers Steve Guinan and Jim Gorman; dancers Shawn Womack and Margot Greenlee; visual artists Steven Fink and Zita Sodeika; musicians Bill Walker and Todd Harvey; my amazing advisors at Ohio State University: Terry Barrett, Michael Parsons, and Amy Shuman; the deeply engaged administrators at the Ohio Arts Council, who have done so much to support the arts in Ohio: Vonnie Sanford, Mary Campbell-Zopf, and Joanne Eubanks, among others.

- to my fellow artists, in the past and the present, traveling the roads of Ohio and beyond. And, most important, to my mentors Imogene Bolls and Bob Fox, two pioneers in teaching poetry in the schools of Ohio, who paved the way for us all.

- to my wonderful colleagues and students at Otterbein College, who have inspired and encouraged my teaching these past four years; and to Leslie, Isa, Jason, Noël, and Noah, without whose love and support none of this would have been possible.

Introduction: To Know Again the World

Relearning Where We Live

How can poetry help students find meaning; that is, how can it help them reengage who they are, where they are, and how they see the world? Second, how can we teach poetry in a more comprehensive way, a way in which each lesson, while self-contained and fresh, also links to a wider strategy of interlocking conceptual and perceptual skills?

This book is woven around these two basic questions. It proposes certain answers, while recognizing the complexities involved with any such answers. It grows out of twenty-five years of trial and error, lessons spun out of necessity and curiosity, as I roved around the state of Ohio, conducting residencies for the Ohio Art Council's Artists in Education program—as well as out of my evolving conviction over that time that students often barely know how to look at where they live.

I've taught in a rural high school, for instance, situated directly across the road from Darby Creek, one of the state's designated Scenic Rivers, guiding students on poetry-writing walks along its banks who seldom had (and mostly *never* had) thought to venture there. I've taken middle school students in Marion—a decaying postindustrial city to the north—on metaphor-scavenging hunts around the blocks surrounding their inner-city school, which might as well have been another planet given how alien and at the same time strangely intriguing they became. Perhaps hardest of all have been the suburban classrooms I've experienced where "outside" is mostly a collection of self-similar streets and cul-de-sacs, leading to the impression that everywhere is the same and hardly worth investigating at all.

This book traces my attempt to find reasons and strategies for guiding students in the reinvestigation of their worlds and their lives, intended for the use of teachers in *all* locations, from the rural to the urban to the suburban. I've grounded the lessons within four interlocking precepts, ones which I've found both theoretically exciting yet adaptable to nearly every grade level:

1. Metaphor constitutes not only the heart of poetry but the core of thought and language as well;

2. Metaphoric thinking roots itself in physical experience—and the more we show students direct ways to link the two, the more their poetry and all their perceptions may flourish;

3. By guiding students in the process of leaping back and forth from metaphor to the physical world, we help strengthen a third and complementary component of thought—*visualization*;

4. Coupled this way, all art, poetry, thinking, and perception offer entrance to a deeply *playful* way of being—not as an escape or mere diversion, but as one of the main routes toward understanding what it means to be human.

There's hardly a lesson here that does not find its grounding in one or more of these ideas. Indeed, I would contend that none of these skills can be fully taught separately. Training in one often enhances facility in the others; and further, I've come to believe that these four skills form a kind of generative cycle whereby poetry might open up and illuminate the "ordinary mysteries" that surround us all the time.

I would hesitate to make anything here into a set formula, a lock-step process to fit every classroom. Rather, these lessons offer possibilities, which perhaps might be useful in constructing your own routes to the aforementioned goals. Mix and match. Use these stories to create your own. Start with evoking your students' *interior lives*—their sense of metaphor, play, and language; their skills in working with memory and invention. Then, wherever you happen to be teaching, guide them out into exploring their world, be that the streets of Columbus or Akron or Colorado Springs, the cliffs of a nearby river valley, the cemetery down the street, or even the local grocery. As a biologist I taught with once put it, "anywhere we are is a habitat of significance," human or otherwise. By connecting their inner sense of perception to the world around them, we can show our students that where they are matters and can become a rich source for writing.

The Structure of the Book

This book falls into two main sections, dividing thirty lessons between them. The first gathers lessons connected to these four principles that I've developed from a wide variety of places and grade levels, including one invented at Thomas Jefferson School, a bilingual academy in Concepción, Chile. Each lesson arises, as I believe all teaching does, from the place of its inception—but I hope they may be adapted for other locations as well. The first half of the book spells out some lessons designed to teach the four skills I've mentioned, in preparation for applying those skills to the investigation of particular places.

The second part lays out a case study—a model that, while intricately bound to the investigation of one place, Mt. Gilead, Ohio, can readily be replicated anywhere. In the fall of 2002, I conducted a three-month residency in two tenth-grade English classrooms of Jill Grubb, a wonderful teacher who contributed greatly to the evolution of each lesson and the residency itself. Mt. Gilead High School is a small community of about four hundred students, located in the county seat of a mostly rural county about an hour north of Columbus. By focusing the second half of the book on this study, in which we deliberately set out to engage these principles, I hope to offer inspiration—and some adaptable lesson plans—for further such studies of how students can come to experience more deeply the rich environments where they live.

By presenting these lessons in a narrative format, often with the names and backgrounds of the student writers included,* rather than in a more generic, prescriptive frame, my hope is that the assignments— and the philosophical principles they contain—will be that much more potable, more adaptable to your own sensibilities and situations. The classroom, the year, and the context may vary, but these interlocking perceptual and conceptual skills will, I hope, be useful to you and your students, wherever you are.

Out of the Poetry-in-the-Schools Movement

Before we begin, let me say a few words about the teaching experiences in which these lessons began—and then about the theory that those experiences evoked.

As mentioned, each of the main ideas here grew out of my travels around the state of Ohio as a "poet-in-the-schools" for the Ohio Arts Council for nearly twenty-five years. What a grand experiment that movement became! Funded by the National Endowment for the Arts, those years resembled a kind of Works Progress Administration for underemployed writers, armed only with our notebooks and whatever sections of our libraries we could cram into our cars. We showed up in classrooms somewhat at random, with neither teachers, students, nor poets knowing quite what to make of each other at first, then slowly warming to the exchange through the creative exploration of language. Pencils moving across the page in mesmerized silence brought a new tenor to the rooms. And the poems that emerged seemed like holy documents, reminding us of some lost elements of our common humanity. I

---

*I have included the student writers' actual first names in most cases.

worked in Catholic schools in Springfield and Mansfield, where the transformative power of symbolism was often no farther away than the ashes placed on their foreheads during morning Ash Wednesday services. I visited high schools in New Washington, Plymouth, and Apple Creek, where driving in I'd need to consult my map to interpret the signs on the nearly empty roads, and cows grazed within sight of the downtown markets. I slept in motels (sometimes donated by local businesses), family bedrooms, and once in a hunting cabin far out in the woods that belonged to one student's grandparents.

Gradually, like so many of the hundreds of poets visiting the schools across the country, through many trials and errors I noticed certain types of lessons and approaches evoked richer poems and contained certain "ingredients" I started trying to name. Nothing sapped a day or a lesson of its excitement more than mediocre poems, and poems without a clever or fresh use of metaphor sapped that energy the most. But how does one teach that essential approach? As with most of us, I struggled to make metaphor's application more than cursory ("the cloud was white as cotton . . . ", etc.). By hook or by crook, as they say, I found that when I brought *stuff* into the classroom, or got the kids moving or connecting their poems to their bodily experience of the world, the writing—and the metaphors—got better. I began carrying boxes of objects from room to room . . . old car parts, pieces of curled driftwood, deer antlers, geodes, a coagulation of melted lead I found outside a factory in Mansfield. Before class, students would often gather around the "stuff table," picking up these items like flotsam from a shipwreck, fascinated most by those objects they could not name. And their metaphors grew. Even when the assignment didn't deal directly with the stuff, having those objects before them in the room gave them imagery from which to draw. As some of the philosophers I read later could have suggested, what else would the students have to make metaphors *from*? Like lamps to our sometimes glazed-over eyes, metaphors can lead us back to an exploration of the senses.

Indirectly, visual awareness slowly began to play more and more of a role. I turned instinctively toward imagery, the first source for my own poetic training. I always knew that poems created mental pictures. But how does one convey that to kids, when they mainly wanted to tell stories and, in adolescence, conjecture about thoroughly abstract topics like the nature of love and the universe? By giving students visual images to spark their own imagination, bringing in reproductions and sometimes artist friends to display their work, or taking kids to nearby museums, it all got richer and more intriguing. Here the ripples widened—and circled back on themselves. For five years I worked in a program called DepARTures at the Columbus Museum of Art, visiting classrooms around the city and then guiding students on poetry-writing tours of the museum. But writing from art alone proved to be empty without first grounding their poems in metaphor and the physical world.

And everything was less exciting without the essential element of **play**; for all theory, all pedagogy, and all *experience* grows stale. I remember listening to yet another group of high school students at Cloverleaf—a wonderful class that had been involved from the start—read their "dream poems" (an assignment I had used many times but was beginning to tire of). Somewhere in the middle, I got a spark: "Let's take all our poems," I said, "and cut them up into some of their most surprising lines, then put those lines in this box, stir them around, and divide them up so we can put them back together again, sort of like an experiment in the collective unconscious." When the combined poems that day proved so much more exciting than our individual efforts, I knew I'd accidentally opened a new door. If I could build assignments that were more like games, and encourage a sense of playfulness with words so that students weren't just out to "write meaningful poems" but let the meaning emerge out of sound, imagery, and play, I was often stunned by how the writing blossomed. But why? Eventually, I sought out answers.

Four Interlocking Theories: Metaphor, Physicality, Visualization, and Play

I went to philosophers, linguists, cognitive scientists, and poets themselves. Could these four skills be somehow related? My reading gradually suggested to me that they were. Here are some of the main supports upon which I base such a claim:

Step One: *Metaphor, so many theorists now insist, sits at the heart of how we speak, who we are, and how we visualize the world.* Robert Frost said so in the 1920s and 1930s—and folks like Max Black, Roman Jakobson, Paul Ricouer, George Lakoff, Mark Johnson, and Giles Fauconnier have since agreed with him in spades. In essence, they claim that how we structure our perceptions is rooted in metaphor, symbol, analogy, and sign— all versions of each other, and means, as Frost put it, "saying one thing in terms of another" (41). In his deceptively homespun way, he was both building a case for poetry and sparking a metaphor revolution that exploded over the next seventy years to reshape our view of the mind.

When we weave in semiotics, the study of how all societies construct themselves around signs—and remember that signs are basically metaphors—we get the feeling that if we're going to teach children how the world works, we'd better give them a solid grounding in metaphor, as Frost claimed. Such is the foundation upon which this book rests.

Step Two: Notice how with that subheading comes the implication that we are walking somewhere, perhaps crossing a stream, looking for stable stones upon which to balance. This simple realization leads to the second key idea: *That exploration in metaphor (which is poetry itself) necessitates building a connection of thought with physical experience.* Philosopher Mark Johnson says as much in his book *The Body in the Mind: The Bodily Basis of Meaning, Imagination, and Reason.* "Through metaphor," he contends, "we make use of patterns that obtain in our physical experience to organize our more abstract understanding" (xv). In so many ways, Frost's own premises show up in Johnson's words. The following sentence, for example, could easily have been written by Frost: "It is not possible to grasp the logic of [a] speaker's argument without understanding the basic, irreducible metaphorical structure that holds it together" (5). Johnson goes so far as to maintain that *all* our metaphors grow out of our bodily, physical experience of the world. I'll say more on his work later, but let's suppose that he's right. What would this mean for poetry? Wouldn't our students' poems get stronger if we involved physical experience in the process? That's been my sense. Maybe that's because we're clueing them in to how the mind works. And what child, if free to explore, can resist becoming fascinated with the workings of his or her own mind? The theory behind this book contends: metaphor grows out of the mind interacting with the body and the physical world—and the physical world, when investigated with curiosity, opens up the workings of the mind.

Step Three: And the visual? W. J. T. Mitchell, leaning on Foucault, claims that "knowledge itself is a 'system of archeological strata made of things and words, of bands of visuality and bands of readability'" (*Picture Theory*, 71). Images matter because they are crossroads of knowledge, the points where the visual and the verbal meet. To physicalize thought is to bring it onto the stage where we can see it as well as say it. Words abstract meaning from experience, but they can't do so without setting up further experiences for us to enter—physically, visually, and by means of sign. Poems are routes into such visual/verbal play, almost as if they were a blend of essays (statements) and paintings (imagery).

We allow students' writing to get richer when we offer them the means of entering that process.

Step Four: Are you following me? We're about to step onto the other bank, the premise of which is: *Societies are visual, physical, metaphor-based arenas of play—and the arts are the source where that play is enacted, where metaphors get unpacked and put together again, and where real change is possible.* One key source here is Samuel Taylor Coleridge's idea of "the Secondary Imagination," which "dissolves, dissipates, in order to recreate" (28) that which primary imagination puts in place (our worlds). A century or so later, Johan Huizinga, the father of modern play theory, claimed that "civilization arises and unfolds in and as play" (i) and calls poetry "a play function . . . that proceeds within the play-ground of the mind" (119). Such play is at the center of how societies operate . . . and if poetry is at heart playful, what then? Biologist Lewis Thomas calls us the word creatures of the planet. Don't we owe it to our kids to help them experience how play operates, how the mind is structured, and how metaphors *play with us*, if we are going to help them understand themselves and the world? In other words, don't we owe them poetry?

Such, in condensed form, is the theory within which this book operates. But don't let me tell you. Let the students show you. For more than theory, more than lesson plans, more than a narrative of one poet's journey through the schools, this book celebrates an array of student poems—and a way of *reading* student poems—which I hope can invite us all to reconsider what poetry can do, and what our students can teach *us* about rediscovering the world.

I Poetry and Perception: Tools for Reengaging the World

1 Awakening Metaphor

Watch, spend time with, and listen to young children and you'll begin to see how much they are involved in metaphoric and playful investigation. When my daughter Isa was one year old, for instance, and playing hide-and-go-seek, she looked up to find oblong dots on the closet wallpaper and tentatively mouthed, "Rain." A year later, peddling her tricycle down the street, she proclaimed, "I'm pushing in summer." Our deaf son, Noah, at age one and a half, tried for a week to balance a gray magnet on the gray fur of the cat—no doubt because her gray fur should attract the magnet just *like* the refrigerator does—and once I watched him try to blow up a long, brown catalpa seed, all the while making the sign for "balloon." "Every child," says psycho-ecologist Edith Cobb in her wonderful study *The Ecology of Imagination in Childhood*, "must integrate a world image with body image in order to know where and who he is. 'Privileged' or 'underprivileged,' every child tries to structure a world" (17). She goes on to claim, as Frost would no doubt concur, that "the recognition of the value of . . . metaphor would seem to be the key to the journey" (25).

With Cobb, I believe that there's a natural poetic or metaphoric imagination in children. Hughes Mearns found evidence for this in the 1920s, as he roamed the country giving talks about literature to parents and teachers. Mothers would approach him afterward to report instances of just such moments of insight and clarity. One is from a girl named Hilda, age three, who on her way to sleep one evening, spoke this:

> I have a secret from everybody in the world-full-of-people
> But I cannot always remember how it goes:
> It's a song
> For you, Mother,
> With a curl of cloud and a feather of blue
> And a mist
> Blowing along the sky . . .

These reportings gave him the idea that children "already have a language adequate for the purposes of their lives, but we do not always recognize it when it appears right before us" (66). Our younger daughter Noël, for instance, sitting outside after dinner one evening when she was three, asked me: "Where does the dark go when the dark goes down?" Minutes later, she couldn't remember her own question, but I believe it was in tune with the intuitive sensibility that has informed poets across the centuries.

Isa, after several months of memorizing haiku from a little book we had, began making up her own. In them I see that same physical perspective on the world as Noah's magnet experiment or Noël's astronomical speculation. In a field, age four, she said, "Here's a poem I made up":

> Under the apple tree I stand
> feeling like a mouse
> for it is my giant

And, weeks later, on a walk in the woods:

> When the leaves fall
> it seems to me
> that the world
> shrinks down.

Notice how *physical* these short poems are, and how much they apply the basic categories of up/down, under/above, and action/response. Mark Johnson in his book *The Body in the Mind* claims such oppositions form the basis for the metaphoric structure of thought. They are tiny sentences that hold her body in place within the moments of her experience. Johnson traces all imagination to the workings of metaphor, and metaphor to the physical/kinesthetic structure of what he calls our prepropositional experience of the world. Building on his previous work with George Lakoff, he claims that this prelanguage realm of the body and its physical environment is all we have to think with—the sense of balance, weight, dimension, and relationship. Just as we cannot fully touch "the real world," we cannot step outside our bodies, or our minds that reside *inside* the body, to get some objective view. To make sense of things, to find that "worldview" Cobb talks about, Johnson says we build elaborate metaphorical structures to interpret and investigate experience. All of these basic structures become the unconscious mental frameworks into which we place our earliest thinking. And such thought patterns don't somehow "go away," or merely disappear into more sophisticated reasoning as we grow older. Rather, they remain as the internal structures around which we construct more elaborate, complicated thoughts. The mind is continually dealing with "where we are now" and shaping "novel orderings" (157), just like Isa walking one evening near Shelby, Ohio, holding her mother's hand and saying, as if she were thinking the world out loud:

> The sun sits
> on top of the sunset.
> The sunset slowly flows
> through the city.

I have to say, until I heard her short poem, I don't think I'd ever really looked at the connection between the sun itself and all that it "sits upon" as it slides out of view.

Metaphor provides our best means of grappling with any new realities we face from early childhood onward. We say things such as "I could see right *through* him" or "That's a lot *closer* to what I meant," or even "Literary metaphor occupies only *a small corner* of the whole realm of what metaphor entails"; phrases that continually refer to our kinesthetic experience of the world. Such images become functioning metaphors and gradually, through the use of repeated experience, metaphors become working schemata, signs, and symbols.

There's much more to say, but that's it in a nutshell. We build our speech and our thought as structures in the air, in the mind, or on the page—whether we do so with playful awareness (as in poetry) or follow some preestablished patterns (as in our daily speech). Notice even in these last two sentences, for instance, how metaphors guide the sense. Johnson contends we cannot understand even the most basic of utterances until we grasp the metaphoric structure they are using. I use a phrase like "in a nutshell" as a common way to say *I'm condensing the thought here* and the phrase "build our speech" as a way to emphasize the active function of thought. We can't get away from such moves (there—do you see?—two metaphoric references in one seven-word sentence!).

Along with Frost, the Russian semiotician Roman Jakobson did as much as anyone to revolutionize our thinking about metaphor. Jakobson likens the process to a huge webbing or a multibranched tree hovering over our thought process; one that the tool of metaphor allows us to figuratively enter. Moving from Frost's inkling that "all thinking is metaphor" to Jakobson's theory of speech being either communicative or associative (see Jakobson on Metonymy vs. Metaphor), then on to Johnson's later contention that all thought consists of metaphors that grow out of our bodily experience of the physical world, and you have a theory that could possibly transform how we teach thinking and imagination in our schools.

Jakobson on Metonymy vs. Metaphor

Roman Jakobson, whose work on metaphor revolutionized the field midway through the twentieth century, broke all speech into the metonymic and the metaphoric. Though many have previously defined these terms as versions of each other, Jakobson sees them taking quite opposite directions—and necessarily so. Metonymy, which can be defined as any time when something replaces some other thing or experience or event, constitutes much of our speech. It "gets us by," allowing us to plug preestablished words or phrases to STAND FOR what we mean, using commonly accepted designators. This is speech's communicative function. We can say "The lamp is on," for instance, and no one is going to question, "on what?" The word "lamp" stands for the object we are all familiar with, just as the phrase "is on" lets us know that it's giving light. Speech act after speech act replicates this metonymic structure. "Giving light," when we think it through, is a fairly complicated process that would take much explanation to convey. Just as a phrase such as "going to the store." Here, we get neither the full experience of "going," nor much sense of what entering that store will be like. We get INFORMATION—and likely, all the information we need at the time. "Going" stands for the multilayered act of finding the keys, walking out the door, closing the door, getting in the car, or heading to the subway, checking the sky for rain or snow, etc., etc., etc. If we included all that in our statement "I'm going to the store," we'd never actually get to GO. Metonymy, Jakobson claims, consists of much more than substituting "Washington" for the whole U.S. government. It substitutes language for experience in order to transfer information quickly from one person to another. Metaphor, on the other side of the scale, conveys relationship and association. It allows us to CONNECT one experience to other experiences, making comparisons and suggesting meaning. Jakobson pictures metonymy as a single-dimensional bridge, or a conveyor belt, one lock-step leading to the next, in order to get from one point to another. When we want to explain, on the other hand, when we want to say what that particular lamp or that particular trip was like, we venture into the realm of metaphor, linking one thing associatively to other layers of experience. (See Hawkes, 77–82)

Lesson 1: Metaphoric Being

Let me provide a very beginning example of metaphoric thinking in action. In one difficult middle school residency, nothing was getting through. After the first day, I was ready to give up. Though these students had volunteered to participate in an extra "writing and art" experience, and though we were grouped in a circle around a table in the art room to open up discussion and help us listen to each other, students were constantly holding conversations of their own and idea after idea would devolve into chaos. Debriefing at the end of the day, the teachers told me "that's just their style," and that the students actually were conferring about the very concepts I was raising, but I wasn't satisfied we'd ever get anything done. After another such day, on Wednesday morning I brought in the wheel off my bicycle and placed it in the center of the table. "What could this be besides a bike wheel?" I asked. Suddenly all the abstract concepts had a *physical presence* to connect to. They came up with many things: a pinwheel, a Ferris wheel, an eye with many parts, a god's eye, a roulette wheel, a creature with many hands. Each metaphor no doubt came from some bit of experience in their own memories, for, as Johnson points out, thinking comes from the manipulation of previous physical embodiments applied to new information. I was glad for this start . . . but I had in mind a further image, one which I hoped would unite this diverse group into a facsimile of a class for the next few days. I said to them, "What if this wheel represented US—this temporary class meeting in this art room for a week?" "Then each of us would be a spoke," one of them said. "Yes," I answered, "And we would spin when all the spokes spun." For the first time, I saw a collective spark in the midst of us. Carrying the idea further, I suggested, "And I am not the center, nor are your teachers here; the real center is whatever we create together. And that circle won't spin unless the spokes work together. Even one 'off kilter' spoke sends the wheel in gyrations." I didn't tell them about Frost's idea that "all metaphor breaks down somewhere" (41); that you just have to know "how far you may expect to ride it and when it may break down with you" (39). I'm just glad they did ride it far enough to make a little more unity in the class for the remainder of the week.

A few minutes later, when asked to make a metaphor for what memory is like, Kristan, an eighth grader, wrote: "Memories are like a forest of the world, trees for each person, some more, some less, for the seasons of the world." I could tell metaphor had taken on a presence in the room. So Juan, who had been struggling to concentrate all week, often volunteering wonderful insights but rarely able to get a whole thought onto paper, wrote this metaphor-based poem while looking at René Magritte's "The Domain of Arnheim" (Figure 1.1):

Figure 1.1. René Magritte, "The Domain of Arnheim"

Trapped in a Shell

I'm in a shell moving around
I hear big bangs
Like avalanches falling from the mountain top
The shell starts to crack
I see light
It was like the moon in a big blue jar
I didn't know what to do
I was scared
It seemed that I have been reincarnated
Reincarnated as a bird
A bird with no fear

—Juan (8th grade/Columbus, Ohio)

At the end of the day, both the teachers and I knew something marvelous had happened in that one period, for Kristan, for the class as a whole—and for Juan. When we went to the museum a day or so later, Juan was one of my allies on the tour, seeking out the underlying meanings in the artwork, writing concentratedly about several pieces in the galleries.

Not every classroom calls for such direct measures, but all might benefit from some hands-on group work on constructing metaphors from objects and the world around them. Here are some ways of applying what happened in Juan's class:

a. Bring in objects—particularly ones that are easily visible by the whole class—for students to sink their metaphorical teeth into . . . either individually, in small groups, or as a class. Even in the midst of other lessons, I've found it useful to remind them they have this skill by playing this way with something around the room or out the window. Poets have learned to do this naturally, as do children who have been shown how to imagine creatures in clouds—but for beginning writers, gentle reminders (and practice) help.

b. Leading students from objects to abstract and mysterious concepts like "memory" or "time" can be a nice next step. Poems can be written creating metaphors for time or fear or hope or poetry itself. Even a quick brainstorming such as Kristan wrote from can provide a gentle reminder for how exciting metaphor-making can be.

c. "Living in a painting," particularly abstract, surreal, or nonrepresentational works, provides a ready means for asking students to invent metaphors for what they see . . . and what it would feel like to be there. The following poems offer two such routes.

Poems for Writing Metaphorically about "Going Inside a Painting"

For nearly every poetry lesson, I recommend the use of model poems—especially ones that stretch the students' sense of what a poem can do. Our days are filled with practical prose, so without *stepping back into what poetic language can do,* how will we remember? In these cases, it may not be so important to understand everything about the poem or to unpack all it is saying—but more to dwell in its sense of mystery, sound, and possibility.

Moving Forward

The deep parts of my life pour outward,
as if the river shores were opening out.
It seems that things are more like me now,
that I can see further into paintings.
I feel closer to what language can't reach.
With my senses, as with birds, I climb
into the windy heaven, out of the oak,
and in ponds broken off from the sky
my feeling sinks, as if standing on fishes.

—Rainer Maria Rilke (trans., Robert Bly)

Oceans

I have a feeling that my boat
has struck, down there in the depths,
against a great thing.
And nothing
happens! Nothing . . . Silence . . . Waves . . .
—Nothing happens? Or has everything happened,
and are we standing now, quietly, in the new life?

—Juan Ramón Jiménez
(trans., Robert Bly)

Also: See "Stone" by Charles Simic on pages 24–25. If one can "go inside a stone," I've often suggested to the students, perhaps one can go inside a painting or a sculpture as well.

Lesson 2: Oppositional Thinking

My contention here is that the arts are our surest way into multifaceted, metaphor-rich thought and experience. I base that idea not only in theory but in my experience teaching children. Consider the following poem by Nicole, a fourth grader at Duxberry Park Elementary. Shown a poem by Carl Sandburg in which he personifies night ("Night gathers itself into a ball of dark yarn . . . / Night speaks and the yarns change to fog and blue strands"), followed by an oppositional poem by Federico García Lorca, "Balanza," where he also speaks of day and night ("Night forever quiet / the day comes and goes. / Night stays dead and lofty / the day contains a wing"), Nicole invents her own oppositions of "tree" and "God" and physically/visually/experientially becomes both:

> I am tree floating in the air
> floating up every second
> but wait I stopped I'm on
> a cloud and looking at
> the world
>
> I am God in stupid tree's place
> and it sure is not a palace.
> I am stuck in the ground
> with nothing to do
> besides growing and growing.

Here Nicole's thought has transcended easy visualizing. It's more like she's in the middle of both her subjects . . . a true "chiasmus," where she's seeing the world from both levels at once. Poet Philip Wheelwright tells us that human experience is filled with such oppositions, "the tension between self and other persons, between self and physical environment, between love and antagonism . . . " (46). True art may well grow out of these realities of experience, which are at once visual and verbal, seen and felt, and, in Wheelwright's words, bear "traces of the tensions and problematic character of the experience that gave [them] birth" (46). All physical experience may well have this push and pull of tension within it, out of which we shape our most meaningful imagery.

This assignment originated as a game my daughter Isa and I played to pass the time on our one-hour trips to her violin teacher's house. I heard one day of someone saying "the opposite of war is . . . fishing" and began thinking maybe we could come up with some of our own creative oppositions. I would give her a word—such as "brick"— and she would give me what one might call a tangential opposite—such as "tooth." The fun was in seeing if we "got" the connection. Sure, there might be a more obvious connection for "brick," such as "feather" or "wall," but it was more fun to see what emerged on that day, at that particular time. Another day she might have said "sun" (as one can imagine the sun beating down on a field of just-made bricks, thus forming something of a visual opposition). We would proceed for 20 minutes or so, taking turns giving the starter word, before moving on to other such games.

It is easy enough then to adapt that exchange to the classroom. I usually go to the board, ask for a concrete word—and then its "opposite"—and students raise their hands with their most immediate answers, continuing with fresh pairings until the board is filled. "Wall – Wind" / "Shadow – Storm" / "Memory – Morning" / "Ghost – Teacher" / "Rain – Ocean" . . . well, you see the scope of possibilities here. Another option, especially with smaller groups, is to play the game "in the air," alternating around the class from row to row. Someone, though, should be recording the pairings, so that they're available for the writing that follows.

After briefly hearing the Sandburg and Lorca poems (see the following sidebar), we each choose pairs of our own with which to play. I've had students veer toward keeping with the same pairings, which they toss back and forth in two-line units for the whole poem, as in:

> Brick shelters its eyes with heavy brows
> Tooth knows another, sweeter sleep
>
> Brick listens incognito when night begins its schemes
> Tooth sautés the memories of its distant birth . . .

And so on . . . the trick is to step out of our normal expectations of what brick, or tooth, or sun—or any of the other mysterious and ordinary components of our world—can do; to imagine that everything can come alive again, filled with the inner nuances of being. I've learned a lot from seeing how far they take these oppositions. Here are two other examples, including a long string of pairings from one student, which she had scribbled all over the page:

> Day as the darkness of night.
> Night in which you see sun rise.
> Day sleeping sleeping
> In night which wind blows away
> to make day come.
>
>   *
>
> Feather weighs
> 1000 pounds
> Brick, not
> knowing where
> to float.

The Night Nose

> The nose stands in the day
> waiting for the night
>
> Pepper sits and waits sits and
> waits in the middle of the sea
> without a boat
> Black stands in the night
> Black hides in the day
> Come out black

 *

Shoe as
high as it
sounds. Cloud,
stomping the
ground.
 *
Goat not hungry at all
Hot dog eating the goat
Goat being the only
creature on earth not
having everything for
itself.
 *
Orange taking "How to be a
  Lemon class!"
 *
Braided, like a twist of lemon in
  your sandbox.
Twisted like the hatred of love
  and the love of disgust
 *
Hunting through the
blizzard so deep.
Peace like a war
departing the wind.

    —Martine (4th grade/
Douglas Elementary, Columbus, Ohio)

Red walks through the desert
Only being noticed as a red
blur as people walk by

      —Caitlin (4th grade/
      Douglas Elementary,
      Columbus, Ohio)

Shaping creative (or tangential) oppositions this way can provide practice in visualizing the world metaphorically. For what is metaphor but the linkage of oppositions and distances? Philip Wheelwright might refer to these poems as "diaphoric," as by simply yoking "God" and "tree" together, Nicole has made a metaphoric comparison that might help us to think about both in new ways.

Two Poems for Writing about Opposites

Pairing poets—and poems—can be a good way of working with opposites as well. Carl Sandburg and Federico García Lorca are about as polar a pair of opposed poets as one can find. Yet notice how they work within a similar territory with the following two poems. Pairing very distinctly different poets, both working within the same subject or territory, can be a way for students to learn there's no one way to approach the assignment. Both of these poems, simple as they are in structure, make the oppositions in the world come alive:

Night

Night gathers itself into a ball of dark yarn.
Night loosens the ball and it spreads.
The lookouts from the shores of Lake Michigan
    find night follows day,
      and ping! ping! across the sheet gray
      the boat lights put their signals.
Night lets the dark yarn unravel.
Night speaks and the yarns change
to fog and blue strands.

                     —Carl Sandburg

Balanza	**The Balance**
La noche quieta siempre.	Night forever quiet.
El día va y viene.	The day comes and goes.
La noche muerta y alta.	Night stays dead and lofty.
El día con un ala.	The day contains a wing.
La noche sobre espejos	Night above the mirrors
y el día bajo el viento. .	and the day below the wind.

          —Federico García Lorca (trans., Terry Hermsen)

Lesson 3: Reading the Window

Metaphor—and physicalized thought—played an equally strong role for Chad, a sixth grader at Savannah Elementary, as he stood before the huge art room window, looking out on the rainy parking lot and hillside at the back of the school. We had just finished reading the following poem by James Wright, with its careful observation, using each of the senses, of all that surrounds him. I quote it in full to show the kind of multisensory model Chad was responding to:

Lying in a Hammock at William Duffy's Farm in Pine Island, Minnesota

Over my head I see the bronze butterfly,
Asleep on the black trunk,
Blowing like a leaf in green shadow.
Down the ravine, behind the empty house,
Cowbells follow one another
Into the distances of the afternoon.

To my right,
In a field of sunlight between two pines
The droppings of last year's horses
Blaze up into golden stones.
I lean back, as the evening darkens and comes on.
A chicken hawk floats over, looking for home.
I have wasted my life.

—James Wright

Without belaboring the oddness of that last line (we did of course speculate on what it could mean), the students and I paid more attention to the way the scene comes to life through the senses and through tiny points of metaphoric surprise. Creative opposition, one could note, rears its head as well (the *bronze* butterfly, the golden stones, the simple act of *leaning back* into the hammock). When I asked them to make lists of their own of tiny surprises and metaphors they could imagine from the scene out the window, most had fun with it, seeing the lights as party hats, the telephone wires as fuzzy worms, and so on. But it was Chad who came up to me, tapping my arm and asking, "Would it be alright if I called that circle in the trees [I had to bend down to look] a 'window to the future?'" "Of course," I said, elated, and ten minutes later he brought me this poem:

(window to the future)

the wind blows
the trees sway
the field is like an airport
and the last touches of snow
lay on the ground
I can barely see the old house on
the hill
through the mist
the treetops touch the sky

and puddles everywhere I walk
there's a hole in the trees that
looks like a window in the distance
the view is silent
the ground is wet
(should I go through the window)

—Chad (6th grade)

I only want to say, along with how visual it is, how sensory his poem is as well. As is so often the case in a good poem, the physical world evokes visual imagery and metaphor, which subtly return us to a fresh evocation of the senses. Without a lot of description, you can almost feel the cold, the wind, the treetops touching the sky, almost put your foot in one of those puddles as he leaps off through the window. How much he exemplifies everything Cobb, Wheelwright, and Frost have been telling us. Like Juan, Chad was having his share of troubles that year, his teacher told me later. Yet his interior intelligence had given him that view of the world beyond the school windows, suggesting his life was on the point of change.

So take a class to a good window anywhere in the school—or step outside! See how many metaphors and similes they can come up with in a set amount of time: ten minutes or a half hour. You can even take a walk around the block, pausing in three or four places to record notes. You can ask them to divide their paper into two columns:

Details—things you see/notice/small descriptions of everything out the window or everything around you . . . Colors . . . shapes . . . varieties . . . pairings . . . Stuff right in front of you . . . or far off . . . Oppositions . . . numbers . . . what's "in the center" of the scene . . . what's peripheral?	Metaphors and similes for things in the first column—or anything else that strikes your eye. Think about each thing as if it resembles something else—as if it were alive —or had human or animal characteristics . . .

I've also found it helpful at times to break the chart into three territories:

Details	Metaphors	Inventions . . . supposes . . . and "what ifs . . ."

The whole idea is to give students the tools for absorbing in their world in ways they might have missed before. Then give them some time to meld their observations into descriptive poems, with themselves at the center of the seeing. I sometimes suggest they imagine the scene in front of them as if it were there at some other time in their lives . . . when something "has just happened," good or bad or in-between. And they don't talk about the event in the poem, but let the mood of that event shape how they describe things. It's a way of bringing in a bit of drama or story into the poem, without letting the poem become merely a story. James Wright's poem is a good example here. We know more has gone on than he's saying, yet the miracle is how much he's made that simple scene come alive.

Look for other examples to include with Wright's to help the students with their own seeing. Gary Snyder's "Mid-August at Sourdough Mountain Lookout" and Denise Levertov's "One A.M." are two possible additions to include here.

Two Poems for Capturing Moments and Scenes

As with Lorca and Sandburg, the works of Denise Levertov and Gary Snyder contrast productively for students. While both frequently focus on "the moment" and well-conveyed scenes, Snyder does so through accumulation of detail, whereas Levertov leans more on metaphoric leaps of connection. Here, she creates a little puzzle—it's often fun to ask students what season of the year she's describing—while Snyder evokes several senses at once in his Zen-like description of all he could see from his mountain lookout. After doing a list such as the ones described in this lesson, it's helpful to offer students two such contrasting approaches to taking in the world:

One A.M.

The kitchen patio in snowy
moonlight. That
snowsilence, that
abandon to stillness.
The sawhorse, the concrete
washtub, snowblue. The washline
bowed under its snowfur!
Moon has silenced
the crickets, the summer frogs
hold their breath.
Summer night, summer night, standing
one-legged, a crane
in the snowmarsh, staring
at snowmoon!

—Denise Levertov

Mid-August at Sourdough Mountain Lookout

Down valley a smoke haze
Three days heat after five days rain
Pitch glows on the fir cones,
Across rocks and meadows,
Swarms of new flies.

I cannot remember things I once read,
A few friends, but they are in cities.
Drinking cold snow water
From a tin cup, looking down for miles
Through high, still air.

—Gary Snyder

2 Embracing the Physical

All thought—from a young child's to an advanced philosopher's—is bound up with our understandings of and associations with the physical world we inhabit. A toddler takes a block and joyously throws it down the stairs, over and over again, partly because "she can," but also, according to Mark Johnson, because the experience of up-and-down is central to her growing investigation of the world. By the same token, we shape complex analyses of society and other phenomenon through up-and-down groupings and what Johnson and others call "image schemata": as in "up-is-good, down-is-bad" or "knowledge-is-like-a-tree" growing toward greater understanding. It would seem then that our knowledge of how metaphor works to enliven and awaken thought should include—and maybe even begin with—connections to the physical objects of the world.

Stories of scientists discovering new ideas through observing the physical world abound: Einstein riding the streetcar and noticing that buildings looked different the faster the speed of the "relative" traveler; Crick watching the bubbles take on the patterns of interlocking spirals in a glass of beer. Poetry has its own history of rooting its "ideas in things" and in our physical experience of the world as a whole. Some students, especially in middle school and high school, consider a page of poetry as a place to deposit their deepest thoughts and emotions, forgetting how often their deepest thoughts and emotions grow out of their experience in the world. The whole thrust of this book is to give them practice in making compelling leaps between all that is around them—the rain, the trees, the chalk, the grind of motors, the stretch of wires down a city block, the dance of a field out toward a hillside—into their own reengagement of the world.

Poetry is not only a means of creating metaphors. Rather, because metaphors are so fundamental to the construction of thought, born as they are from the physical realities of the world, poetry, as the art of the metaphor, is a way for students to regain a sense of wonder about the world. When we shape a fresh metaphor—in a poem, a novel, an essay, in a painting, or even a conversation—we establish a relationship to a world. Consider this paragraph from the middle of Harriet Arnow's *The Dollmaker*. In it Gertie Nevels, a woman from the hills of Kentucky transported to the tenements surrounding the factories of Detroit, ponders her doll-carving in the late evening light:

> The hard white light overhead hurt her eyes and made a shadow on her work. The night sounds of Detroit came between her and the thing in the wood, but worse than any noise, even the quivering of the house after a train had passed, were the spaces of silence when all sounds were shut away by the double windows and the cardboard walls, and she heard the ticking of the clock, louder it seemed than any clock could ever be. She had never lived with a clock since leaving her mother's house, and even there the cuckoo clock had seemed more ornament than a god measuring time; for in her mother's house, as in her own, time had been shaped by the needs of the land and the animals swinging through the seasons. She would sit, the knife forgotten in her hands, and listen to the seconds ticking by, and the clock would become the voice of the thing that had jerked Henley from the land, put Clovis in Detroit, and now pushed her through days where all her work, her meals, and her sleep were bossed by the ticking voice. (210)

It is a world of THINGS that is evoked here, things with resonant meaning. Things that are both physical objects and that place themselves in the fictional environment so that the fullness of their sensory momentum shapes Gertie's world for us. Even nonentities take on a physical presence here, such as the "spaces of silence" in the evening that "shut away" all other sound. Our realities—personal or public—are composed of such spaces, which in turn determine relationships. Arnow's world unveils itself as a kind of fictional illustration for Mark Johnson's concepts of physically based thought, a thought fully cognizant of the presence of the thinker/the perceiver's body.

William Stafford gives us a poem that in a similar, quiet way links what poetry does to a desire to reach back into the elemental aspects of the world. In it he touches on many of the concerns of this book, while evoking much of what Mark Johnson says about the embodiment of thought.

Evening News

That one great window puts forth
its own scene, the whole world
alive in glass. In it a war happens,
only an eighth of an inch thick.
Some of our friends have leaped
through, disappeared, become unknown
voices and rumors of crowds.

In our thick house, early evening
I turn from that world,
and room by room I walk, to

enjoy space. At the sink I start
a faucet; water from far is
immediate in my hand. I open our
door, to check where we live.
In the yard I pray birds,
wind, unscheduled grass,
that they please help to make
everything go deep again.

This is precisely what I think poems are about: projecting us back, via words, into an elementary (and elemental) reengagement with being, whether that "being" consists of a memory from deep back in childhood, a scene out on a city street, a pair of shoes, or a hammer, or the physical realities of mountains, rivers, stars, and volcanoes. My experience in schools tells me that kids hunger for these sorts of connections, but that too often these are missing from the curriculum of study. That too often basic *wonder* is missing, as facts are accumulated, assignments lined up and checked off, principles conveyed. Perhaps one of the things art does—whether it's poetry, theater, painting, music, or dance—is place us (either as observers or creators) "at a point of vibrant intersection," to use a phrase Richard Poirier constructed as he described the way Robert Frost's poems so often put us "in the middle of a field." How often do we see Frost, in his poems, exploring, in equally philosophical and physical ways, some "element of earth"? Can't we make such experiences available for students as well? Recently, two of my college students were working with a group of seventh graders over the course of a whole semester, receiving much resistance and do-we-have-to-do-poetry-again looks *until* they took a field trip to explore and write poems in a local cavern. After lunch, they spent a chilly April afternoon sitting around a bonfire they'd built (mostly to warm up) and writing about . . . what else? . . . the fire in front of them. Only *then*, my students reported, did their commitment and connection to poetry become real. If we can find ways for students to physically engage with the mysteries of the world, then maybe poetry can take on more meaning in their lives.

Lesson 4: Objects and Riddles

Here are two quick exercises, or games, for grounding students' beginning experiences with poetry in metaphoric observation of what is right around them.

Riddle Game for Objects #1:

The first game starts with showing the players (aka students) a page of riddle-poems from around the world. The first are from the Kuyukon tribe, northern Canada. I tell the kids about how such riddles were made—often in the dead of winter, as a kind of entertainment, pre-TV. Someone would make up a riddle, as condensed and suggestive as possible, often for a living creature, as these two are, so try to guess:

> Far away,
> a fire flares up.
>
> (a fox's tail flicked upward in the middle of a field)

> Flying upward,
> ringing bells in silence
>
> (butterfly)

Give them clues and have them guess. Usually the guessing illustrates the process of gradually narrowing the possibilities—from bird to bee to kite and finally to butterfly.

It's a reasoning process, with all the qualities of a game. What's odd is that it often takes as much time for adults to get these as it does third graders! Here are three more, taken from Andrew Welsh's book, *The Roots of Lyric*, in which he traces the beginnings of poetry back to riddles, proverbs, and chants, offering examples from around the world (25–46):

> Behind the village sit those who have donned
> white handkerchiefs
>
> (from Romania—for fence posts topped with snow)

> Father's scythe is hanging
> across mother's Sunday skirt.
>
> (from Sweden—for the crescent moon)

> That which digs around
> In the deserted village
>
> after that which is lost)
> (from Ghana—for the heart, which is always searching

The next step is to try some ourselves. I usually make up a few ahead of time—such as this one, for something that can be found in nearly any classroom: "Three disconnected boxcars" or "Night has left its shacks/ at the edge of the black lagoon" (for three erasers lined up on the blackboard ledge). Or "In the ice, they have drilled/tiny breathing holes for the fish" (for random patterns of dots that often can be found on many schoolroom ceiling tiles). We then send a couple of students out of the room and make up a room-based riddle or two for them to guess. They work on these together until they get a way of phrasing that gives enough hints without revealing the answer too obviously. It will take them a few tries to get the hang of this sort of riddling—they need to keep at it until they are only using metaphors in their clues, leaving out such lines as "It's red and it has stripes . . . " or rather, transforming them into "He bleeds so evenly in rows . . . " The central move here may well be a matter of personifying the world. Then bring the volunteers in and begin the guessing. You might even set up an ongoing contest to see who can come up with the best riddles for the classroom over the course of a semester.

Admittedly, this sounds like a game more suited to the elementary school classroom, but I've adapted it for graduate workshops in museums, choosing a gallery of more abstract sculptures and writing an example riddle for one piece that tries to convey something of the artwork's essence without limiting its open-endedness. This provides a good icebreaker as participants try to guess, while at the same time teaching a lot about how metaphors work. Group members can then spread around the gallery to create their own.

Riddle Game for Objects #2:

For this second game, gather a bunch of interesting, ordinary objects from around your house, garage, basement, or yard. The object can be anything that is not too "pretty" or plastic, but rather has layers of functionality and use, from an old rusty broken hammer head to a well-worn drip-stained paintbrush, a partially unwound skein of yarn, a piece of twisting driftwood, etc.

Schoolrooms tend to be so dominated by characterless objects— formica-top desks, bland or colorless cement-block walls—that any infusion of difference is welcomed by the students. As I noted earlier, I sometimes bring a box of objects even if we're not specifically going to write about them. I'll tell them that poets like to *look* at things, the way the well-known artist Georgia O'Keeffe used to bring shells and bones back from the desert into her house to inspire her paintings.

So sometimes the objects are just there for "something to look at," which might inspire an idea in a poem on quite another subject, but sometimes I ask students to choose an object and, after talking with them about metaphor, ask them to make lists of all they see in it, as if they were going to write a poem about it (which we also sometimes do). I say there is no need here for complete sentences yet, just intriguing images and phrases they get from thinking in expansive ways. As in (for some dried river reeds): "What if they held the mind of fire?" or (for a blob of coagulated lead): "It could be the puddles left from the silver moon." Such phrases can push past simply saying, "It looks like . . . " or "It seems as if . . . ," but both formats are useful.

Two things can happen next. You can gather their lists, choose overnight the most suggestive ones, read a selection back the next day, with those objects displayed before you, and guess. Secondly, you can look at some object poems (such as Charles Simic's "Stone") and ask students to grow their lists into full-fledged poems. In this latter case, they can try to disguise their objects into riddle-like poems, or not, as their impulse directs them.

Two Poems for Writing about Objects

After listing as many metaphors as possible for a particular object, here are three poems for weaving those notes into full-fledged poems. Simic takes an imaginative route "into" the object, almost from a dream-like stance. For older grades, I've sometimes shown students my own poem about some bagworms I once noticed while sitting beside a river, pointing out how I just poured as many metaphors and similes as I could into the lines, hoping to convey a feeling of claustrophobia—a sense of being inside that miniature world.

Stone

Go inside a stone
That would be my way.
Let somebody else become a dove
Or gnash with a tiger's tooth.
I am happy to be a stone.

From the outside the stone is a riddle:
No one knows how to answer it.
Yet within it must be cool and quiet
Even though a cow steps on it full weight,
Even though a child throws it in a river:
The stone sinks, slow, unperturbed
To the river bottom
Where the fish come to knock on it
And listen.

I have seen sparks fly out
When two stones are rubbed,
So perhaps it is not dark inside after all;
Perhaps there is a moon shining
From somewhere, as though behind a hill—
Just enough light to make out
The strange writings, the star-charts
On the inner walls.

                                —Charles Simic

Bagworms in Their Tent above the River

                    Reversed architecture, translucent
        spun body: from where I sit, like a worshipper,
                the sun lights up your tunneled womb
            encircling, honoring even, the leaves and limbs
                which you destroy. Thickets of tiny worms
        collect in the pockets of your tilted circus home—hardly more
            than hairs crawling, burst down the narrow, swung arches
                    like ringless, leaderless thieves.
        I have burned your kind before, in my early age,
            stripped web from orchard notch with a gasoline glove,
        sometimes a single apple, like a distant tumor
        inside a breast, hanging within your ghostly
    elegance—or plunged the whole lopped branch into the burner,
a kind of hellish pleasure in the shrivel of those
            death-hands as they climbed the black walls
    of the flames and fell back in. Is yours
        the same feast, though slower, more attentive and content,
            branch by branch the tree stripped down
                within your sealed city? One loose coil of a child
                    falls from a strand, lost it is
    and nodding at the wind, one tipped finger
        on the farthest ivory key that finds it has moved
            beyond the realm of sound, where another weaver
        slides through the silk to drag it safely in—
as the thick of the fire hauls back
        each orange and bickering tongue.
        Beside you the scourged branches of a previous
            victory hang, black and peeled, blistered raw,
                still rippled with your sting.
            And already in this enclosure the bones of leaves
            hold their scoured forms, dull lamps
    or limbs off a fetus born without a spine. Like them,
    I could not slay you, though I lived within,
            eyeless bodiless emperor who even now
                releases spy-spores toward your next reunion,
                summer by summer will never let us out
        of this gorgeous, breathless, woven room,
        without edge, without beginning.

                                —Terry Hermsen

Three Students' Riddle-Like Poems about Objects

First I felt cold,
and I was all white.

Airplanes fly over me a lot,
but they don't touch me.

The rain falls heavy at night,
And I stand there and shiver.

I have some company, now and then
but lots of times I'm lonely.

I get poked by being climbed,
but my cover always grows back.

Now and then I shiver
from cold, but I always stand.

The wind blows fearful
and the snow never melts.

I look down on the city below,
and I do not tremble.

—John (4th grade/
Butler, Ohio)

(a mountain)

I am a string being
pulled from
both sides
      I don't want
to be pulled,
      yet by being
            pulled, I tie
your life together

I am a string
      I was made
from the wool
      of something greater
and more powerful
      than I

I am a string
      being tied
in knots by
      those that
            rule me
My knots, though,
      sometimes are
intertwined
      with my thoughts

—Caitlin (9th grade/
Lodi, Ohio)

(a teenage daughter)

born in a shell, which has taken the credit,
the birth of a shape,
the crack will not destroy but bring a fine meal,
maybe life with a little bit of time,
from the barnyard creature, quite humble indeed,
white with a wobble and a splat when
dropped,
morning drowsiness, with the beam of light,
the king of stones . . .
warm in the hay

—Mike (7th grade/
Cloverleaf Middle School)

(an egg)

Lesson 5: Metaphor and the Body: Sports Riddles

I often begin this next lesson by showing the students how much language itself is rooted in metaphor. Back in the 1950s, poet John Ciardi often made the point that all words are metaphoric at root, and it's not hard to see he was in many ways right. Take "pandemonium," for instance, Milton's made up word for the chaos of hell, linking "pan," which is Greek for "all," with that more ominous word "demons." What could be clearer? Ciardi also points out that the river Meandros in Asia Minor gave us "to meander" (like an old-bed river), and that "shambles" came from the name for that area of certain European cities where the butchering was done, the leftover parts falling to the ground "in a shambles." As words emerged to name experience—and as they continue to emerge—what else do we have for the naming but connections to other places and experiences? So "astronaut" is a combination of "star" and "sailor," so to "imply" is to "layer in." So "curfew" is a blend of "cover" and "fire," referring to the Medieval laws that required villagers to cover their fires at night to prevent burning the town down. Look up "cloud" in a good-sized dictionary and you will find this word derivation: "Old English: "clüd" = "rocky mass or hill." How very playful such a naming is, linking the hard solidity of a mountain to the oppositional billowing of a storm front! Again, when we try to name the nuances of things and experiences, we search for connections to help bring them to life . . . and we enter the metaphor hardly knowing what our language is doing, based as they nearly always are in physical realities.

Poetry helps us reenter our language—and our experience of the world—in a more direct or "inside" way. For some students, sports are a good place to begin, for they include both inner and outer realities. Think of the excitement and the sense of power when spiking a volleyball, or the struggle of moving through a mass of uplifted hands when catching a pass in football or basketball, or the quiet drama of lining up a particularly tricky pool shot, or the sense of "disappearing" into another realm we get when diving into a swimming pool. I often show the class David Allen Evans's "Pole Vaulter" for its careful attention to the inner sensibilities of the sport. I've never pole-vaulted—but somehow after I read the poem, I feel like I have! We look at the way his line breaks tuck in and turn, the way one's body would when springing up and through that exhilarating arc. His poem makes only the slightest use of direct simile, but is somehow deeply metaphorical at base, in quite another way.

Next I show them an exercise of my own, in which I have taken each small motion of a particular action in a particular sport and ask the students for guesses as to what I might be doing. It's odd—I've had some fourth-grade rooms where the first or second guess is right, and others (even in high school) where we have to read the poem several times for the clues to sink in. Nevertheless, the exercise of working our way through each nuance in the action seems useful for slowing down the mind.

The writing assignment then is to take some other action—from a sport or everyday life (we often list these)—and think our way through them on the page. For the first stage of the process, I suggest they follow Evans's lead, reentering the moment or the motion with as much slow-motion care as possible; then, as they write their poems, replace each stage of their imaginings with metaphors for "what it feels like," ending up with a riddle that the rest of the class might guess.

Pole Vaulter

The approach to the bar
is everything

unless I have counted
my steps   hit my markers
feel up to it   I refuse
to follow through
I am committed to beginnings
Or to nothing

planting the pole
at runway's end
jolts me
out of sprinting
I take off   kicking in
and up   my whole weight
trying the frailty
of fiberglass
never forcing myself
trusting it is right
to be taken to the end
of tension   poised for
the powerful thrust to
fly me beyond expectation

near the peak
I roll my thighs inward
arch my back   clearing
as much of the bar as I can
(knowing the best jump

Riddlesport

I begin to bend
as if I were going to tie my shoe,

and stop, like a tower that stops
just before falling,

then sway back, my toe pointed
forward and arched
as if I was going to trip someone.

And while with my left hand
I slowly offer a drink to the sun,
I swing my right arm back & up
as if it were a loose pole
connected to a pin on my shoulder.

Above my head again it
stops, as if I were pointing a dagger
down at my head,
jerking forward—

like a sledge hammer hitting the water
or as if I were handing a paper
to the king.

—Terry Hermsen

(a tennis serve)

can be cancelled
by a careless elbow)
and open my hands

    —David Allen Evans

Poem-Riddle

Like a dancer's
own style
whipping, turning, fast, slow.
Some good, some bad.
Back and forth like a pacing soldier.
The floor being striped in
uniform style.
Parallel.
When you come to the end
you must start again.
But you leave your mark as you go.
No one's the same!

    —Katie
    (Buckeye Valley HS)

Enigma

The sphere of gold
is launched in sacrifice to the sun

It is forced out of orbit
by a jealous renegade

who has muscled his way
into the atmosphere in hopes that

he will land with the world in his
hands

    —Krista
    (Elgin HS)

Riddle

I early race to my goal,
as a starving man to food.
I reach out with my right hand,
grasping the handle, as if it were
  gold before me.
My head slowly bends down
like I was praying to some ancient
  God.
The crystalline arch reaches ever
  upward.
My mouth opens as if in awe.
I bow like I was the star in a play,
and I begin to drink.

    —Josh
    (Elgin HS)

Everyday Riddle

My foot raises
Like an airplane taking off
And bends like a flamingo resting
In cool cool water

It comes back
And lands
In front of
The other

Both still at first
Then moving slowly
But in a rhythm
Moving
Moving

Two submarines
Floating, speeding through
Water as if it were air.

    —Rob
    (Edison Elementary)

Answers:
Top left: writing Top right: having your shot blocked in basketball Bottom left: getting a drink of water Bottom right: walking

Lesson 6: Chainsaw Inquiries

Johan Huizinga, the founder of modern play theory, sees "poetry . . . as the stronghold of living and noble play," particularly when "civilization as a whole becomes more serious—[when] law and war, commerce, technics, and science lose touch with play" (134). Such was the case in Poland in the middle of the twentieth century, when the reigning dictatorship made free communication of ideas nearly impossible. As Huizinga could have predicted, poetry was one of the last spaces left for playful undercutting of the status quo. Witness Tymoteusz Karpowicz's poem, "The Pencil's Dream" (1957), a clever commentary on the society of the times:

> When the pencil gets ready for sleep
> he firmly decides
> to sleep
> stiffly and blackly
>
> He is helped in this
> by the inborn
> inflexibility
> of all the pith in the world
>
> The spinal pith
> of the pencil
> will break
> but cannot be bent
>
> He will never dream of waves
> or hair, only of a soldier
> standing at attention
> or coffins
>
> What finds its place in him
> is straight, what is beyond
> is crooked
> Good night
>
> —(trans. Czeslaw Milosz, 100)

Could the messages in this poem—about breaking boundaries, about the metaphorical dimensions of "waves and hair" have been said in any other way at the time? It's unlikely. So childlike, the poem seems almost inoffensive, yet it undercuts the state agenda in a most telling way. "The Pencil's Dream" reminds me of Huizinga's rhetorical question: "Is not all personification from beginning to end a playing of the mind?" (139).

As in board games or sports, we need rules in poetry to make the game work. So say Cacciari, Chiara Levorato, and Cicogna, in their wonderful study of "Imagination at Work: Conceptual and Linguistic Creativity in Children": "Individuals—be they children or adults—if not provided with specific environmental constraints follow a 'path of least resistance,' that is, they retrieve a specific instance of a given category and pattern the new creation after it" (157). As the surrealists discovered, and as I suppose Huizinga would agree, the "game" and the intricacies of its rules create the energy in the new work. The more concise and the better-chosen and invigorating the rules, the more possibility there is for fresh discovery.

Here's such a game based on the following poem by Ohio poet Jeff Gundy:

Chainsaw Inquiries

What do chainsaws love?
>Lumber. Dust. Live wood pulled down
>by the dying. Sun on last year's leaves.

Do chainsaws share a hidden fear?
>Rocks. Nails. A few, older, fear
>their appetites, and that what they chew
>does not nourish them.

If chainsaws dream, of what?
>Of hands that never tire, tanks
>that never empty. Forests
>rising quick as grass. A heaven
>where silence never falls.

Do chainsaws share a secret grief?
>They cannot hold what they eat,
>cannot keep what they kill.
>They cannot feed themselves. (25)

We could talk about this poem for some time, with all its clever commentary on our overconsumptive society. For now, it's the framework Gundy provides us that matters. For could we not take anything, and by asking some basic questions about it—using a twist on the old personification technique—see something fresh inside it, and in ourselves, as does Columbus high school sophomore Amanda in her poem:

Questions for Water

Can water feel a heartache?
>Heartbreak is water's dependency. It
>lives to soothe our pain.

Does it cry when misunderstood or mislead?
>Yes, it pours upon the shore its
>salty ache.

Is water always smooth or are there
rocky roads along the way?
The rocky roads are hidden as makeup
hides a woman's wrinkles.

Can water feel & taste & look alike?
All water is born on different shores.

Here, what could have become a sappy poem about lost love and the distance between people becomes a playful construct that takes our old clichés and lets us walk within them, feeling the links between oceans and heartbreaks, life-maps and wrinkles-in-skin, and (in the wonderfully evocative last line) the distances between nations and races and our own private desires.

You and your class can try this also. First, list objects from everyday life on the board. Then draw out some thoughts about how much of our lives are made up of these objects. You might at this point read "The Pencil's Dream" to get them into that playful mood without which much poetry is not possible. Could we not regain a sense of the world we had in childhood—and which many cultures throughout history have strongly maintained: that all of the world is alive with possibility? (Again, Charles Simic's "Stone" might be a good poem to bring into this discussion.) Finally, look at Gundy's poem and talk about some of the nuances involved. With high school students, you can ponder what a chainsaw represents, as if it were a symbol of our times. With younger students, they can simply enjoy the way Gundy gets us thinking like a chainsaw . . . and go on to invent their question-and-answer poems.

Ask each student to choose an object from or feature of the world and write out five "personal" questions about it, pretending the object had emotions and memories of its own. At this point, each writer can answer their own questions—or, if the group is fairly cohesive and trusting, pass their questions to a partner and answer each other's, as did Jill Grubb and Cindy Fidler, teachers in a workshop I conducted at the Ohio State University in Marion:

What do watches do at night?
Snore softly at first, then loudly.
Dream of being fast forwarded.

Who are their relatives?
Strings, rubber bands, sands, and shadows.

How do they celebrate their birthdays?
With an extra hour of sleep,
Polishing cloths, oils, and a new band, a diamond hand.

Where do they go when they die?
To the jewelry box next to the single earrings & Grandma's
Hummel brooch with the eye missing.
There they turn their faces to the wall.

What do they desire?
Grit remover. Sweatless owners.
Worldwide travel. Syncopated rhythms.

Do they remember their births?
Do you?

  —Cindy Fidler and Jill Grubb
   (teachers, Mt. Gilead High School, Mt. Gilead, Ohio)

3 Training the Visual

To teach poetry in our time is to grapple with how images are created and processed, in our individual consciousness and in society at large. Poems that don't create pictures in our minds run the risk of remaining in the abstract. And yet our world—and especially that of our students—is so filled with images! How can we expect them to *get* poetry if we don't show them how poetry and the physical world are intricately linked? If we don't see ourselves climbing the trees in Frost's "Birches," or the world swirling out of control in Yeats's "The Second Coming," it's doubtful we'll make much meaning out of those poems—or any others. And from a writer's side, it helps to imagine (and to have practice in) our words creating pictures in the reader's mind. Metaphors, at the same time they are intricately linked to our experience of the physical world, are equally tied up with making visual images. It is to this third arc of my argument that this next section of exercises now turns.

Poet after poet in the twentieth century has probed the interchange between visual and verbal imagery, starting with William Carlos Williams and Rainer Maria Rilke. Both studied hard the work of sculptors and painters, talking with visual artists, aiming in their poems to catch, in Rilke's case, the spirit of a panther in words the way Rodin might in bronze; and in Williams's case, to make poems that might move with unmediated commentary, to be pure form, a record of "the thing itself." Wallace Stevens, Frank O'Hara, and Denise Levertov—poet after poet as the century unfolded sought to make a "moment in the world" stand fresh before our eyes. In a way, each poem worth its salt gives us a "way of seeing" itself, of entering the space it evokes that is particular to that poem or that poet, that does more than *describe* but rather conjures what it might have been like to be there. For a very straightforward but at the same time very meditative example, you might have students take another look at Gary Snyder's "Mid-August at Sourdough Mountain Lookout" (30). Influenced by Buddhist philosophy as much as or more than modernist aesthetics, Snyder's poem nearly removes the self—gives us that world from a high vantage point, the quick sensory details yielding a presence that can almost be inhaled. By bleeding most of the verbs out of the poem, Snyder emphasizes the thing-ness of all he sees, the way Williams sought to do. This world is as sharp and clear as its language is. It's full of facts, with just enough adjective/verbal flourish ("pitch glows") to awaken each of the senses.

The same could be said for Yeats's "The Second Coming"; it opens up a world that we need to learn to see. Yeats doesn't "back up" to give a suitable explanation for where we are going; no, we are thrust into a world we can hardly know, until we start to swim with the images. Here's the opening:

> Turning and turning in the widening gyre,
> The falcon cannot hear the falconer.

This is more symbol-based than the Snyder poem. At least we question more whether we are to picture a *real* falconer, or a kind of god-like figure trying to control the world. Still, the central image of chaos continues:

> Things fall apart, the center cannot hold,
> Mere anarchy is loosed upon the world.
> The blood-dimmed tide is loosed, and everywhere,
> The ceremony of innocence is drowned [. . .]

Again, we're clearly in a more symbolic land than "Mid-August. . . ." No calm drinks of snow-water here. Yet we are asked just as powerfully to invent a place from which to see this world. We must play with the imagery, we must make sense of whatever the "blood-dimmed tide" might conjure.

The same could be said for the poems of Issa and other classical Japanese haiku poets. Pick up Robert Hass's insightful translations and notice how each poem creates a little symbol—a reference to a perceived or invented world—an entrance back into that world (the way a painting can bring back a historical period . . .). It is, then, something of a "visual art." It's certainly a lot closer to a painting than writing an editorial or an article in an encyclopedia. The philosopher W. J. T. Mitchell and others have claimed that the strict divisions between word and image, visual and verbal, may be too arbitrary anyway. We might more accurately think of a continuum of images, ranging from the graphic to the literary. Mitchell says that images can act as "something like a character on the stage of history" (9). Think of the mental picture we create when we hear the name Hitler, for instance. Or Charlie Chaplin. Or the Black Death. Find a painting of a pilgrim in the 1600s, pull up a photograph of a Dust Bowl refugee from the U.S. heartland in the 1930s, conjure an image of a hitchhiker in the 1960s—you have images which would evoke a time period, which indeed moved *through their times* as "figures" that directed thinking.

Mieke Bal, the Dutch art historian, has argued for just such an awareness of the *interplay* between text and image. "'Verbality' or word-ness," she says, "is as indispensable in visual art as visuality or image-ness is in verbal art" (212). A painting does not exist *purely* in the world of paint, but in our dialogue with that paint. *We read the visual clues of a painting,* says Bal, *and we visualize the images of a written text.* What could be more useful in helping students make use of the multilayered ways we *see* the world through words and pictures?

There is, however, a bit of a fly in the ointment here, for the power of representation, on all fronts, from the visual to the verbal, has grown immensely in our time. Everywhere there are images for us to emulate or critique or absorb unthinkingly. The power of received images—from TV, from advertising, from movies and posters, and even from our own photographs—has become so strong, some have said, as to erase what-ever actual connection we may have once had with a physical, perceiv-able world, and replace it with one where images are constantly being manipulated. Mitchell, following Baudrillard and others, calls ours an age of "hyperrealism," in which the *real* is so easily manipulated that we can hardly tell the difference. He gives the example of "Disney-world's wave pool [which] advertises itself as 'better than a day at the beach'" (*Picture Theory*, 358)—and one could posit dozens of other examples to symbolize how the fantastical *fabrication* of worlds has replaced a more physical *investigation* of the world within our daily con-sciousness. Yards become lawns, animals become cartoon characters, meals become packages, and the weather becomes something we watch on a screen, removed from anything we might significantly touch or experience deeply. Can we blame our children for being as disengaged from actual experience as we ourselves sometimes are?

I would argue that one of the educational tasks of poetry in our time is not only to help students understand the workings of metaphor and the conveyance of physical experience onto a written page, but a deep grappling with how images are created, with how they affect us—and thus, how the triangulation of experience ➔ word ➔ image can be reentered and reclaimed for our own deeper understanding.

Perhaps an image would be appropriate here? Pieter Bruegel the Elder in the sixteenth century gave us a powerful illustration in his draw-ing of Elck (see Figure 3.1) of how we are constantly *looking* for, but not always finding, self-understanding. The scene is of a man hunting through an array of trash, full of baskets and lanterns and chessboards and bundles, with versions of himself everywhere—playing tug-of-war, hiding in a barrel, disappearing in the distance on some sort of journey.

Figure 3.1. Pieter Bruegel, "Elck"

And central to us is one version of Elck, peering like Diogenes into a lantern, as if to discover something significant. Behind him is a frame for a painting, at the bottom of which are the words (in Dutch): "Nobody knows himself" (Stechow, 26 and 29). The implication is that even in 1558, when this work was done, thoughtful people knew the difficulty of breaking through the mess of the world, through the stereotypes and illusions, to a stronger sense of what it means to see ourselves.

Art can be a great instructor. And writing poems about paintings and other visual media can be a fine way to awaken our students' sense of imagery. Perhaps most of all, such assignments can provide us with occasions to awaken in students how images of all kinds work, how they can be manipulated, and how we can gain new power over them once we make them our own—through writing.

Lesson 7: A Voice in the Painting

Shifting to the visual side of my argument, I must make a confession: I find teaching students to look closely at paintings a difficult task. So many layers must be crossed—from the ahistorical sense of the young

Figure 3.2. Gerrit van Honthorst, "Samson and Delilah"

writer to a painting, say, from 500 years ago to the sheer overload of visual information a painting often gives us and the limited vocabulary most students bring to their seeing. Yet I believe the process is worth it. If Mitchell and Foucault are right that knowledge is woven from "things and words, from bands of visuality and bands of readability" (*Picture Theory*, 71), how can we not make the effort to show students how to read this rich metaphorical world?

Let's take as an example a poem by Steven, a fifth grader in Columbus, Ohio, some years back, whose poem about Gerrit van Honthorst's painting, "Samson and Delilah," reveals a student's engagement with physical reality (via a painting) and of the way the awareness of the body can shape seeing (see Figure 3.2). It may tell us something about the issues involved in writing a poem about *anything*, and in trying to define—or refine—what we're asking students to do when they engage with the arts.

The scene is: Clinton Elementary on the near-north side of Columbus, and a fifth-grade classroom, again rather noisy. As a visiting poet meeting the kids for a second time before they go to the museum to write, I toss out the idea of writing in the voice of someone in a portrait or other scene with people. Larger than most of the kids, Steven sits at the back of the room, near the teacher's desk. As you will be able to tell, his spelling is atrocious—though some might describe it as unique. With no prompting or extra information from me, he selects a reproduction of van Honthorst's painting and takes the view of Samson (see Figure 3.3).

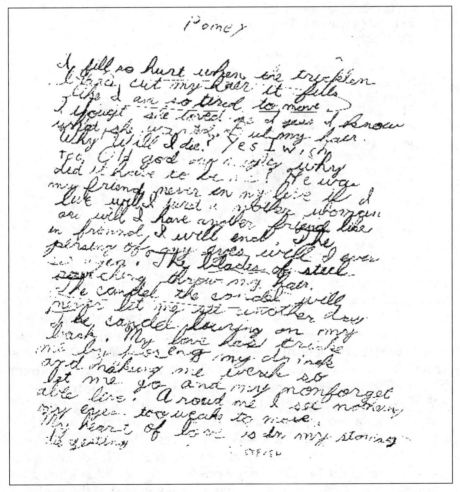

Figure 3.3. Steven, "Pomey"

First, let me translate Steven's poem into slightly more conventional English (while keeping some of his inventions intact):

Poem

I feel so hurt when the tricklen
blades cut my hair. It feels
like I am too tired to move.
I thought she loved me—I guess I know
what she wanted. But my hair.
Why? Will I die? Yes, I wish
to. Oh God almighty [old god our mighty] why
did it have to be me? He was
my friend. Never in my life if I
live will I trust another woman
or have another friend. Like
in friend, I will end. The
piercing of my eyes—will I ever
see again? The blades of steel
ranching through my hair.
The candle, the candle will
never let me see another day.
The candle burning on my
back. My love has tricked
me by poisoning my drink
and making me weak. So
let me go and my nonforget-
able life. Around me I see nothing,
my eyes too weak to move.
My heart of love is in my stomach
digesting.
    —Steven
    (5th grade/Clinton Elementary/Columbus, Ohio)

This poem contains so many lessons about how to help students reengage the world, the world of paintings, or anything else. First of all, Steven seems to have *entered into* the painting and participated in it. In a complex way, he's *projected* himself into another person's experience, in the classic poetic manner of taking on the persona of what he is writing about. Furthermore, he has *looked*, in that he has used terms from the painting itself—the candle, the comb, the drink. Clearly, he has brought some knowledge to the work, particularly of the story being portrayed, knowledge probably gained from home or church, and he's able to bring that previous knowledge to investigate a new situation.

Secondly, his poem creates an emotional event more than a descriptive one. In the interior monologue he imagines what's going on inside Samson's brain, and he's caught some key part of the *emotional essence* in the painting. Much of this he accomplishes through *metaphor*, in a rather stunning way, at the end. "My heart of love is in my stomach digesting" takes a fresh turn on an old phrase, and he doesn't mouth the cliché—he transforms it, sending the heart down into the stomach, implying that the poem itself—or this monologue—is a way of digesting what has gone on.

In keeping with Mark Johnson's ideas about metaphor and thought, he physicalizes the painting. The strengths of the poem are in the *physical, kinesthetic details*. This may be where the heart of his understanding lies. We feel more fully the candle burning on his back, or the comb (here a fierce symbol of control and deceit) "ranching" through his hair, or the poison circling through his body. It is a despairing *voice* we hear, almost as a physical presence, wandering around in our heads. The poem is more than words on the page—they seem to happen, as Frost said such lyric or theatrical poems do, "in a character, on a stage, in a setting." *And quite inside us!* They suggest that to write a poem—about a painting or anything else—is to hear the phrases internally, as if we were walking through whatever subject or material we have before us.

So how to apply what Steven has taught us here? One suggestion would be to collect a series of portraits from various time periods. They can be photographic, painterly, or even sculptural, or visit a portrait gallery in a nearby museum. Any image of a person in a scene will do, and the more evocative the better. Talk about why humans have made images of ourselves—and even about the various societies that have forbidden the representation of the human face and the human form. At all ages, discussion of what we see in the "mirror of art" can be fascinating.

Then collect some "portrait poems." In Steven's class, we read John Haines's "Leaves and Ashes" for an example of evoking a character in a scene. Other good choices would be "An Old Photographer from Vermont" (see p. 131), or Sandra Cisneros's prose-poem, "Salvador, Late or Early," or James Wright's "Milkweed" (see p. 150). You might suggest that the students take some notes about their person first—what they see and what they can invent. Then write a poem that is either "about" the person in the scene, "from" the voice of the person (as Steven's is), or "to" the person (in the form of address or an ode). Studying portraits is very much like looking in the mirror of humanity, a mirror that tells a story and suggests realities below the surface.

[Note: Other ideas for writing about visual art can be found under "Museums" in Lesson 14 and in Lessons 22, 28, 29, and 30.]

Lesson 8: Kid Talk/Art Talk: Learning to Listen to the Students We Teach

This lesson is a chance to pause and reflect on our students' lives, and mostly, I want here to tell a story of a boy named Philip (not his real name—though he himself is quite real). He's the sort of child that drives teachers crazy, picking at the edges of their school days like a pesky mockingbird at the edge of an orchard, constantly provoking disorder in the room. The distinguishing feature about Philip is that he is never still, physically, mentally, or verbally, at least if left to his own devices. This is a story of frustration—but also one that raises the flicker of hope.

Philip joined a group of six students who were meeting with me at an elementary school library in Columbus one afternoon in late April. After spending three days in their class during the winter as a guest writer, prior to their poetry-writing field trip to the Columbus Museum of Art, I was back at the school on my own volition to "get to know the kids better," asking them questions about their lives—where they played, what they loved or feared—and wondering how their view of things connected to the world of art and poetry. I had brought bottles of water (it was already hot that spring) and cookies to ease the flow of conversation. The first half of our time was spent talking about their lives. The talk was jazzed, productive, interactive—and noisy. And Philip was the source of much of the latter. Whenever someone said anything, Philip had a joke to follow it—sometimes humorous, sometimes cruel, but always undercutting. When I mentioned, for instance, that we would get to something "in a minute," he jumped in: "Did you say 'Eminem'?" (I assumed he meant the rapper, not the candy.) When Victoria asked me, "Do you remember my name?" he chimed in with the song lyrics, "Say my name, say my name. . . . " His mental and conversational life seemed to be one rejoinder after another—he was king of the outside reference—to the point where we ALL got tired of it. When Julia spoke of her scariest time as being this whole school year, when three people close to her had died—one in a freak accident when a bulldozer crashed over a hill where her cousin was playing—Philip had to undercut *that* too, faking false tears and making us all turn on him in disgust at his insensitivity. I should have asked him to leave. Much of the time, I felt like doing so. But then I wouldn't have gotten the conversation that follows.

Philip, it seems, knows no boundaries. His mind is always "at play" and seldom "on task," except when we turned to looking at art (see Figure 3.4). Listen to this exchange as we discussed Gustav Klimt's "Baby (Cradle)":

Figure 3.4. Gustav Klimt, "Baby (Cradle)"

Terry: What do you think this painting is about?

Philip: I think it's about . . . about . . . a bunch of . . . somebody made a quilt or something . . . and they put it all together . . . and they put it on the baby.

Zack: I think he's in bed . . .

Chad: And that's the pillow . . .

Terry: What's the feeling? What's the painter getting at?

Chad: He's sleeping and he's trying to go to bed . . .

Jake: He looks like he's really sad.

Terry: Why do you say that?

Jake: He looks really happy (inexplicably reversing).

Terry: OK, why do you say happy?

Jake: Because from this angle he looks like he's smiling.

Terry: This is weird . . . I mean . . . there's this huge amount of clothes with just this little tiny baby . . .

Philip: I think . . . I think . . . that the baby . . . that it's ('cause I don't know if it's a he or a she) . . . looks like she's dreaming . . . she has all these covers and this is the clouds—and she's floating on air . . .

Terry: Cool, so it's this baby's dream of all this wealth and stuff . . .

Philip: Ya . . .

Terry: That's pretty neat . . .

Philip: Like a . . . like a . . . princess . . .

That moment changed my life in terms of thinking about what art can do for kids.

Ironically it was only later, listening to the tape and hearing how quiet things got at this point, that I realized something quite significant had happened. (At the time I was mostly frustrated with Philip's constant interrupting.) For in that quiet I began to see Philip's mind as a playful mind; one so thoroughly engaged with an active, interchangeable world of ideas and words that he can never stop—*until given a reason to.* If we had been dancing, he likely may have been the one to keep us all in motion. If we had been acting, he may well have played any character, but we weren't. We were, as in so much of school, sitting still. How does a child like Philip learn to channel, as they say, all that energy? Does he simply, as many might prescribe, need more Concerta or Ritalin? I don't want to minimize the very serious problems students like Philip come up against every day in school. But if we squelch that energy, make it sit still always and learn mostly how to take tests, etc., how do we make sure that we don't drum metaphor and playful thought out of him as well, or crush the child dreaming on top of that huge quilt? For you will notice that in those moments of insight, he's tapped into all the qualities we've been talking about here: metaphor especially, along with visual and physical projection.

So what's the "lesson" here? Maybe it's just to take time to listen as well as to seek out ways to help the students listen to each other. Put some paintings up. See what the students say. Break them into small groups and ask them to describe and then interpret what they see. Stress particulars. Add a dash of metaphor. This book is for the Philip in each of us, asking: how might we bring the metaphoric, playful, physical, and visual sides of the mind and the child, so richly a part of what the arts teach and what human consciousness is based on, into more productive functioning within the school environment? It wants to be part of a nationwide effort to make schools more physically engaging, more visually rewarding—and at the same time more deeply engaged with thought. In other words, more filled and engaged with art.

Lesson 9: Housemarks, Doodles, and Inkblots

Along with writing from paintings and photographs in museums and books, it's exciting to search for ways students can write from visual images they create themselves. I have, for instance, spent a number of sessions in various locations visiting art classes, where we arranged their current works around the room and wrote about them just as we would in a museum.

In other classrooms, I've tried out having them make images on the spot, or had them write from images I had made ahead of time. After all, visualizing is visualizing, and the more students hone their skills for bridging the "complex interplay" in one media, the more they should be able to do that in others.

In brief form, here are three examples:

Housemarks

Have students take a look at Conrad Hilberry's "Housemark" poems, which in general offer a fun way to play with metaphor in relationship to visual symbols and forms. It's also fun to learn about the use of such symbols in medieval towns to indicate what house or business sold or made which products. The next step is for the students to make their own "housemarks." The trick is to avoid ready-made visual clichés, such as arrows, hearts, and crosses, but rather to work with basic lines to shape something new (see Figure 3.5).

Doodles

For this lesson I often put on some music and give students time to doodle before they begin to write. As a self-confessed telephone-doodler I suggest four simple rules for "the true and arcane art of doodling": (1) don't try to make your doodle look like anything; (2) use simple shapes and lines; (3) apply continuous and inventive repetition to these beginnings, enjoying a particular line or shape until you feel like varying it; (4) let the feeling of the music guide your hand.

It is sometimes helpful to model this process on the board. I often hand out photocopies of Paul Klee's imaginative drawings, which go beyond doodle but contain a similar playfulness (see following example in Figure 3.6). I give students ten or so minutes to complete their sketches. Doodling encourages students to follow—and to value—their own spontaneity.

When they have filled a page or two with doodles, I read them two example poems. I ask the students how William Stafford's "Smoke,"

The Chevron

This is my sign, the pitch
of my tent on low ground.
It is the march up the mountain
and the march down. It is
a crossroads without a choice.
It is my past and my future
leaning together like cornstalks
after the rain . . .

—Conrad Hilberry

The Frying Pan

My mark is my confusion.
If I believe it, I am
another long-necked girl
with the same face.
I am emptiness reflected
in a looking glass, a head
kept by a collar and leash . . .

I am both the egg
and the pan it cooks in,
the slow heat, the miraculous
sun rising.

—Conrad Hilberry

Figure 3.5. Hilberry, "The Chevron" and "The Frying Pan"

—drawing by Paul Klee
("The Elated")

Smoke

Smoke's way's a good way—find,
or be rebuffed and gone:
a day and a day, the whole world home.

Smoke? Into the mountains I guess
a long time ago. Once here, yes,
everywhere. Say anything? No.

I saw Smoke, slow traveler, reluctant
but sure. Hesitant sometimes, yes,
because that's the way things are.

Smoke never doubts though:
some new move will appear.
Wherever you are, there is another door.

—William Stafford

Figure 3.6. Klee, "The Elated" and Stafford, "Smoke"

—doodle by Terry Hermsen

The Message

Kneel before the voice of wind—
Piano song of snakes and fire

The child is at the steps,
    going down sleepy

Hang up your boat—
    it will make a better roof

Past the river of three,
    Under the horn of the thorn balloons,

Through the cobble of the shell
    and the tiny eye—

There is a way home

    —Terry Hermsen (based on previous doodle)

Figure 3.7. Hermsen, "Doodle" and "The Message"

although not based on the Klee drawing, could be a verbal representation of it. Then I read them my poem "The Message," based on my own doodle (see Figure 3.7). Much as with a riddle, it's fun to discuss how various lines in the poem refer to different details in the drawing. (Again, I see this as a step toward writing about creating metaphors from visual art of any kind.)

With these two models in mind, I send the students back to their own drawings, suggesting they list down the side of a new page some metaphors for what they see in their drawings . . . and then to begin a poem. I suggest that they need not use everything in their lists; rather, let the brainstorming of metaphors be a catalyst for getting them to look closely at their own drawing. The artwork itself may quietly dictate how to begin the poem. Here are two examples in Figure 3.8:

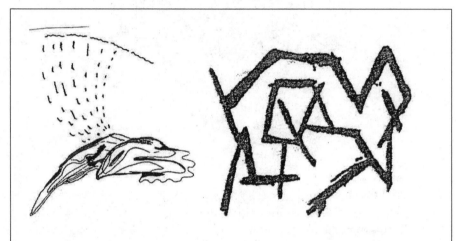

Doodling

Go up the mountain
From here to there
Fall down the mountain
From when to where—

Go up the mountain
Look at the stars
And watch the sky
Light up from glitter.

   —Doodle & poem by
John (4th grade/
Duxbury Park Elementary/
Columbus, Ohio)

The Maze

   Maze through the
shadows and no way out.
   Crossing through
darkness never to be
seen. Cage, cage as in
dungeon far in a castle.
   Chinese writing,
not understood. A
Creature biting at my
Feet. A storm and bow
   to stop it from
killing our people
seeing the bubble
success. In a trance, no way out. Freckles of
a poor girl wishing for
food. Not knowing where
to run after the messages
ran out. Death in the
darkness too hard to see.

continued on next page

Figure 3.8. "Doodling" and "The Maze"

Figure 3.8. continued

Wavering softly in the
night, seeing the path and
glory. Ha hey, ha hey,
is that the land or is that
the thing that killed
my brother 10 seas ago?
Strange mountaintops
nowhere to be found. I
think I know what I
see but then again I
don't. Bugging me like a
fly in my ear. Wind
blowing, not sure, to be
a turncoat or a
stranger, believing in all
just to
get it your way. Eye
of a king, no a
sorcerer, no, a tooth! Dirt,
only knowing the sounds
gush and disgust.
This is my story of
a long time
ago.

—Doodle and poem by Martine
(4th grade/Duxbury Elementary/
Columbus, Ohio)

Inkblots

In many ways a variation on the above two exercises, this lesson uses the medium of inkblots to evoke imagery and story. A few days ahead of time, I make some inkblots myself, using India ink and some fine, absorbent paper, and after they have dried, bring them for the students to choose. I've also made slides of a sequence of inkblots and had students jot down quick metaphors or lines for them on cards, then collecting those lines into group poems, as in Figure 3.9 on page 50:

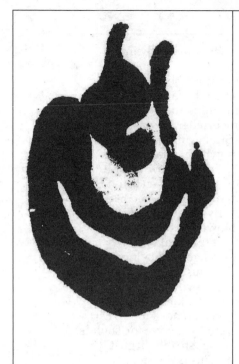

Lines from an Inkblot

A person dying in the mountains
*

Like a baby in a mother's belly
*

A bridge tipping up for a boat
to go through
*

A man bending over
making candles
*

A monkey on a branch
A boomerang in the sky
*

A cat curling and sleeping
*

A man in a tight place
An animal after it's born
*

A clown's make-up smeared
after a rain storm
*

A guy who is cold and
is holding up a feather
*

An old person looking
through opera glasses
*

Like half a man bowling
*

A dog rolling
A cloud going away
*

A snail making his get away
from the prison of his shell

    —Group poem
    (5th grade/Edison
    Elementary/Edison, Ohio)

Figure 3.9. "Lines from an Inkblot"

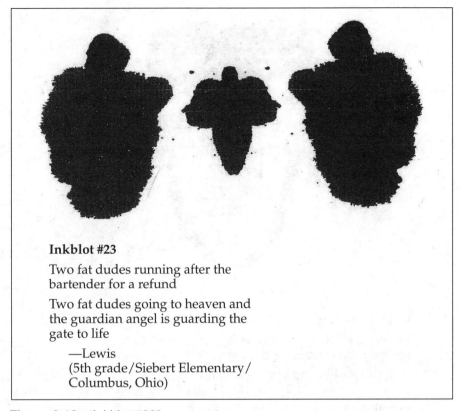

Inkblot #23

Two fat dudes running after the
bartender for a refund

Two fat dudes going to heaven and
the guardian angel is guarding the
gate to life

   —Lewis
   (5th grade/Siebert Elementary/
   Columbus, Ohio)

Figure 3.10. "Inkblot #23"

For example poems, I've sometimes used an inkblot poem of my own,
just to show another option—one drawn from this particular medium
(see Figures 3.10 and 3.11).

Mr Double-Eyes

All skulls, all shovels, all shields
double. All swimmers. All minds.

Even this shabby cap of Mr. Double-Eyes'
that drapes his head like muskrat hides

and allows him to pretend to think—
or see—his upper set of pupil-less flickers,

his cortex slumped
to a flimsy tongue

dividing his pointy lobes. It's like
he perches—as we all—

upon his nobler self—or selves—
the push-me pull-yous

that rock within our sea of worry
and wonder at our troubled nights,

and do their twinned and starry best to shine.

—Terry Hermsen

Figure 3.11. "Inkblot #2: Mr. Double-Eyes"

4 Learning to Play

For many years the conviction has grown upon me that
civilization arises and unfolds in and as play.
　　　　　—Johan Huizinga, *Homo Ludens*

Only when love and need are one,
And work is play for mortal stakes,
Is the deed ever really done
For Heaven and for the future's sakes.
　　　　　—Robert Frost,
　　　　　"Two Tramps in Mud-Time"

Here we come to the final section of theory-based lessons, coupling all the work we've done with metaphor as linked to the body (and with the visual imagery growing out of such a coupling) to our last component of the poetic process: play. Play has long seemed to me to be essential to the teaching and writing of poetry. Whether we are setting up a lesson or tackling a new poem on our own, we have to get into a "ludenic" mood (to borrow Huizinga's term) to even come close to feeling the art. To remain in the realm of practical language and thought defeats us before we even get off the ground. We have to put away thoughts of what to get at the grocery store or the upcoming test. Through whatever means we can muster, we have to enter into a field of invention, of pretending, of speaking in other than our usual voice. If that isn't close to the child who is dream-playing in the backseat of the car and talking of her plastic ponies changing colors because they have eaten the "magic grass," or the one riding her red tricycle down a root-splintered sidewalk playfully laughing that she is "pushing in summer," then I sadly mistake what poetry does. As the poet Donald Hall says, poetry brings "the metaphors of the forbidden child into the words of the rational adult, making a third thing which enlarges human consciousness." In poetry, we don't have to choose between a child's view and the adult's. Rather, they unite. I don't want to pose a kind of hierarchy here, where childhood is poetic and adulthood is not, merely to suggest that one thing poetry can do is tap into the playfulness we had as children—and to suggest that even children today can use a new introduction to the joys of that sort of play.

But how? Particularly when we grow out of those early childhood years, can *play* still be a resurgent force, one that can shake up the rigid role and thought categories of adolescence and adulthood—the clichés that can entrap us into limited ways of visualizing and experiencing the world? For all our love of games, it seems we've come to devalue play in our times. Recesses in our elementary schools get cut back or eliminated. Children's out-of-school lives get scheduled down to the minute with "purposeful" activities and sports or channeled into electronic games formulated by others for their entertainment. Even the root meaning of the word "ludens," which at one time meant being "very playful," has attached itself more to being "ludicrous"—ridiculous or laughable. We tell someone to "go fly a kite," if we want to say how useless they are; we urge them to "stop playing around" if we want them to pay attention to what *really* matters. Just as we've often treated metaphor as a term of embellishment rather than of meaning-making, so we've treated play as something childish or flippant. Yet there is some indication that play may go deep into who we are as human beings, and into the evolution of human communication and thought, as Huizinga's quote above indicates. My own contention is that poetry is "essential play," play—as Robert Frost put it—"for mortal stakes." My concern here is with how we can open up some of the essential aspects of poetry through play. Play as it lets us back into the roots of metaphor, as it flips language on its head, and as it helps us revisualize the world. How can we bridge the gap between our common uses of wordplay and its potential function within human thought and living?

I'm of the belief that play, along with metaphor, is one of the *change agents* within life and language; a play that is not just "wild" but instead operates between "what is set" and "what might be." Such a spark of artful playfulness may be seen in even the shortest of poems, as in this well-known haiku by Joso:

> Snow drifts down
> all the day long.
> Earth has vanished,
> leaving only sky.

Or this, by Basho:

> That summer moon—
> it made me wander
> around the pond all night.

What joy there is in both of these. Yet rather than being mainly "goofy," much of the play in poems of this sort is carefully *planned*. Perhaps play is just that: the space between what is planned or required in our lives and how we live them. Poets often "toy" with our response this way, the line breaks serving the same function that timing does in everyday speech and in jokes in particular.

It's no surprise then that many writers, artists, and even scientists speak of returning to a kind of child-like mind when they are in the midst of their work. Philosopher Gregory Bateson touches on this in his "Metalogue: About Games and Being Serious," one of a series of recorded philosophical conversations with his daughter. In answer to his daughter's question as to whether their conversations are "just a game," and whether he is "just playing around" with the questions he asks and his sometimes evasive answers to hers, which frequently get them into what they've come to call "muddles," he comments, "I think that the muddles help. I mean—that if we spoke logically all the time, we would never get anywhere. We would only parrot all the old clichés that everyone has repeated for hundreds of years" (16).

Of course her next question is, "What is a cliché?" In his answer, he refers to its origin in the realm of early printing presses in which commonly used words and phrases were kept on their own readily usable bars. This is what we're doing much of the time, he says, plugging in "ready-made sentences" to substitute for thought. "In order to think new thoughts," he continues, "or to say new things, we have to break up all our ready-made ideas and shuffle the pieces" (16).

Such is the sort of *playing with* mode of perception that poetry and visual art thrive on. In art, we can consider the givens of our lives and rename them, re-question them, make jokes about them, and distort them. Such play may well be a version of metaphor, but to my mind it's useful to see a certain style of perceptual distortion as pre-metaphoric. A child can, for instance, look at a crowbar and ask the following intentionally goofy questions about it, as in this short poem by a fifth grader in Columbus:

To a Crowbar

Can you crowbar
yourself open?
Why are you named
a crowbar?
If you are a crowbar,
are you a crow?
Is your mother a fork?

    —Maleak
    (5th grade/Columbus City Schools)

No doubt there is visual-metaphorizing at work here. But it's also simply playful. The third question, for instance, "If you are a crowbar, are you a crow?" is more wordplay than metaphor. We need this stage of thought in order to tip things out of the rigid grid by which we look at them. Many of our visual habits are as cliché-driven as our verbal ones. We need to do something to reenter our habitual spaces, to pick up our ordinary "things," and flip them on their heads. I want to believe that there is an area of playful visualization that students can enter into on a purely experiential level that eventually will deepen all of their thought. Only then is the realm of metaphor fully accessible.

Along with turning things on their heads, the poetic style of play, as I've been saying, needs a framework of rules—even if they are self-invented or arbitrary. A well-constructed poetic "game," and the intricacies of its rules, can create energy in the new work. The more concise, better-chosen, and invigorating the rules, the more possibility there is for fresh discovery. We've seen this under Lesson 6 already in the "rules" set up for us by Jeff Gundy's poem, "Chainsaw Inquiries."

But here's another example in Figure 4.1, from fifth grader Byanca in Columbus, Ohio. Within the context (the frame) of René Magritte's "The Beautiful Relations," she takes the very rule-based form of a pantoum and uses it to "play her way into" the painting. In this poetic form, which was invented as a group-poem technique in Malaysia, the second and fourth lines of each stanza are repeated as the first and third lines of the next stanza, with new second and fourth lines being added for each stanza as the poem proceeds. (Note: a full description of pantoums can be found in *Teachers & Writers Collaborative's Handbook of Poetic Forms*.) The poem can extend quite a while, but in common practice ends at the fourth stanza, using the third and first lines of the first stanza as the second and fourth lines of the last:

> When she cries it rains.
> She talks to the world
> Her nose smells the smoke in the air.
> She knows the war is bad.
>
> She talks to the world
> And she cries and she talks too.
> She knows the war is bad.
> She eats the city, my part, my part.
>
> And she cries and talks too
> But she knows she has to do it
> She eats the city, my part, my part
> And the balloon talks to her

Figure 4.1. René Magritte, "The Beautiful Relations"

But she knows she has to do it.
Her nose smells the smoke in the air.
And the balloon talks to her.
When she cries it rains.

　　　　　—Byanca
　　　　　(5th grade/Columbus, Ohio)

Nothing would require Byanca to take on the role that she has in this poem in which she adds in the war or the "eating" of the city. The assignment was merely to write a pantoum about a painting, repeating certain lines according to the pattern provided—a very rule-based structure. Yet it is her sudden personifying of the face in the sky—and her own personal connection to the city below—that makes new meaning out of the work. And I would contend that as we look at a painting, or write about nearly *any* experience, there's always an element of "playing around" or "playing a role" that helps us leap past merely a straightforward reporting. We will see much of this kind of playfulness—and playing within the rules—in the assignments that follow.

Lesson 10: A Table at the Surrealist Café

Many years ago I ran across an article in *Teachers & Writers* magazine that shifted how I saw the poetry classroom from a solitary place based mostly in careful attentiveness to language and toward an active space where we can sometimes achieve as much through playing with ideas *together*. In it, Ron Padgett described how two surrealist poets—a Belgian named Achille Chavée and a Frenchman named Raymond Dauphin—invented a game in the 1930s that opened up routes into questions and other two-line pairings arising from subconscious and random connections. The results often stun a class. How can random connections create sometimes more exciting lines than ones we consciously plan out? No one knows, but the exercise can often turn a sluggish class into a poetry-rich one and a strong class of poets into even more curious and inventive writers.

I often talk first about the nature of surrealism and how it arose from the Dadaists's violent reaction against the horrors of World War I. If this is what Western "reason" creates, the Dadaists felt, and if art is a part of that structure, then something must be done to break the cycle. Their efforts soon fizzled into complete chaos, but the surrealists continued on in a similar vein, because they were sure there were layers of wisdom and life-energy below our conscious minds. Their games go a long way toward proving the point that not freedom alone but freedom-centered structures are what poets often need. I'm not saying we should revert to strict forms like sonnets and sestinas—though practice in such structures can be useful at an advanced level. Nor would I be on the side of those who emphasize simplified forms such as cinquains and diamontes, which constrict students' ability to bring meaning to their poems. Rather, I'm after a useful balance between play and constraint by tossing in well-placed boundaries around their play intended to spark fresh connections. (For instance, I once asked students to include the word "glass" in a dream poem assignment, a move which gave them an impediment around which to weave new imagery.) As the two examples in the previous chapters show, René Magritte's paintings are often good reminders of what "the juxtaposition of *very* unlike things" can do to take thought beyond the easily metaphorical and into the realm of beauty and surprise.

The format for this surrealists' game is simple. One person writes three questions along the lines of "What is . . . " or a phrase beginning with something like, "If _____," or "When _____," and a partner responds with an answer or corresponding phrase in the form of "it is_____," or "then_____," however, neither knows what the other is writing. Questions and answers are then read in the order they were written, listening for the way one tangentially or illogically connects with the other. Not always are the pairings stunning, but they are often so—and enough of the time to truly surprise us.

Stress that the players know what format the other is using, otherwise a much more Dada-like chaos ensues. Then enjoy the sort of "rhyming" satisfaction the pairings create. Perhaps there's some sort of poetic intuition at work. There are some partners that seem to evoke the strongest sort of extrasensory perception. But I've also observed my friend, poet Stuart Lishan, have people line up to answer at random to equally exciting results.

Stress also the variety of play available for each phrase. One can make them as simple as "What is war?" and as elaborate as "What is the flower that swallows its own heart?" Looking at a few of the examples is usually enough to reveal the wide range available within these restrictions.

"Dialogues"—a Surrealist game
Raymond Dauphin & Achille Chavée
Wooden Leg Café, May 18–19, 1938

C: What is a mirage that turns into reality?
D: Time ticking away.

C: What is the character we carefully hide within us?
D: A table with no glass on it.

D: What is a solution?
C: It is the digging of a tunnel under the Channel.

What is a monkey on drugs?
It is the devil with sunglasses on.
          —Chris/Latoya

**

What is the butterfly's color?
It is a golden ring around the moon.
          —Kristen/Jennifer

**

D: What is a river flowing upstream?
C: It is a fly playing the accordion.

D: What is potluck?
C: It is the destruction of concrete data.

C: What is an attempted crime?
D: It is as bland as an English tune.

**

Other formats:

D: When time stands still
C: The forces of nature turn into laboratory jokes.

D: When a star dies out
C: The eyelashes of anger flip coins.

**

D: If art remained the only reality
C: There would be something new at the end of the planet.

D: If everything got settled my way
C: There would be trouble at the Wooden Leg.

C: If our dreams were filmed
D: The eel would coil around the knife.

—translated from French by
Nicole Ball (and originally
published in *Teachers & Writers
Newsletter*; used by permission)

What is the snow when it rains?
It is the girl waking up from
the call of her name.

—Nick/Dominique

**

What is laughter?
It is the man jumping the Grand
Canyon on a skateboard.

—TJ/Gerri

**

What is a fish with no scales?
It is the glass window
scraping against my skin

—Rickey/Katie

**

What is a teacher teaching only one
person?
Water which you drink but then you
see its shadows.

—Taft Middle School
Marion, Ohio
Mary Hardgrove's class

Susan Stewart on Nonsense

For Susan Stewart, in her book about and titled Nonsense, *play—in the form of
nonsense (which would correspond to what we often call "playing around")—
sets the boundaries of culture, for it establishes what does or does not "make
sense." In one culture, for instance, dressing up as monsters and goblins and
knocking on neighbors' doors for candy, the way most communities do in the
United States, is "just plain fun," whereas setting up lights in a cemetery and
decorating the graves of ancestors in a joyful spirit of celebration for a "day of
the dead," as is common practice in Mexico, would be seen as quite outside the
normal. There is, Stewart contends, a boundary of sense that runs at the edge*

of every culture. We test that boundary through play with varieties of "non-sense," leading to a compelling thesis that playing is a constant, if invisible, factor in helping to define sense itself.

"The rules for conceiving reality are constantly in process," says Stewart. "Once other levels of living become readily incorporated into the everyday lifeworld, once they are taken for granted, they become, so to speak, 'dead metaphors'" (40). Such give-and-take occurs at all levels of society. Agreeing with Coleridge, Stewart sees art's role as giving us alternative worlds that can play with the givens we find ourselves in. She says:

> *Art . . . presents a model for interpretation, for arranging perception, which . . . does not so much make its members 'see into the life of things' as it enables them to remake the life of things. (24)*

Nonsense, like art, can shake the presupposed assumptions we boundary ourselves with.

Lesson 11: Jabberwockies of Our Own

In his brief but explosive comments in Chapter XIII of his *Biographia Literaria* in defining the role of the secondary imagination, Coleridge posits:

> The primary IMAGINATION I hold to be the living power and prime agent of all human perception. . . . The secondary I consider as an echo of the former, coexisting with the conscious will, yet still as identical with the primary in the *kind* of its agency, and differing only in degree. . . . It dissolves, dissipates, in order to recreate. . . . (272–273)

Future commentators have made much of Coleridge's distinctions here, claiming that primary imagination is the basic, daily operations of the mind as we pick and choose between categories of our given words and concepts, with secondary imagination's job being, as Nathan Scott puts it, "to unfix and then to refix that which the Primary Imagination has already fixed—in cliché."

We all need, periodically, to have the world flipped on its head, even arbitrarily, if we are to learn—again and again—the nature of the extra-ordinary in the ordinary.

"The poet's job," Terence Hawkes puts it in his summary of Jakobson,

> as one who works with language the way a painter works with colour—requires him to refuse to permit [the] anaesthetic [of ordinary language] to operate. . . . What is important in any poem

is not the poet's or the reader's attitude to reality, but the poet's
attitude towards *language* which, when successfully communi-
cated, 'wakes up' the reader, and makes him see the structure of
his language, and that of his 'world,' anew. (70)

Contemporary poet Stephen Dunn says something very similar when
he claims that although "poems must be clear, by which I mean they
must repay our attention to them, they shouldn't cover territory that's
already clear. That's banality and platitude. *They must make available the
strangeness that is our lives*" (20, my emphasis). Funny, *strangeness* is the
very term the Russian structuralist Viktor Shklovsky uses when discuss-
ing the *why* of poetry. He says that its one central role is "that of 'mak-
ing strange' . . . to counteract the process of habituation encouraged by
routine everyday modes of perception. We very readily cease to *see* the
world we live in, and become anesthetized to its distinctive features.
The aim of poetry is to reverse that process, to *defamiliarize* that with
which we are overly familiar, to 'creatively deform' the usual, the nor-
mal, and so to inculcate a new, childlike, non-jaded vision in us"
(Hawkes, 63).

Isn't this, then, the very process taken by Liese, a fifth grader at
Mansfield St. Peter's Elementary, who, after being introduced to Lewis
Carroll's "Jabberwocky" and his wonderful portmanteaus (*brilliant* +
light = *brillig*; *slither* + *lithe* = *slithy*), invented her own word structures
to make meaning.

Arunning Raway

The dumble fays and drampen bugs all occupy themselves,
While me and the fudwas play in the sun.
And the cooperdops and the riddledoos sing in the grass,
But the world is flippied and damzled about.

I flip down on the crench and the doon is down,
But I haven't gone home.
Dother and Mad come out to lind me,
And I ralk faway to the stream.
Mad has guven ip,
But I reep kunning.

Somewhere, outhere, there's a place for ye and mou,
But I don't wunderstand and I don't even care,
'Cause someone's gonna come lookin',
Someone's gonna see,
That right where I'm astandin',
I'm stayin' here forever.

　　　—Liese
　　　(5th grade/St. Peter's Elementary/Mansfield, Ohio)

Liese's poem plays wildly with the categories of "here and there" (becoming "outhere") and you or me (becoming "ye and mou"). I love how she switches relationship roles, "Dad" becoming "Mad" and "Mother" becoming "Dother." In some way I can hardly explain, I'm *awakened* by her poem the way Coleridge says we are by art. And that's what I'm after: the way art awakens objects to our lethargy; the way it shakes us into hearing words again, to knowing the strangeness, the distance between ye and mou, and the deep wish we all feel at times to "run away;" to make something else of our lives that have become too stale and routine.

It may be that Liese has tapped into something of what Donald Hall, quoted earlier, calls the "forbidden child" here, claiming her own right to decide "where [she is] astandin'."

Here is a second example of a sound-based, Jabberwocky-influenced poem. On the same day that Liese wrote her "Arunning Raway" masterpiece, Ivanna wrote the following poem based on the same assignment, but very different in its approach and effect. She told me afterwards that she imagined it being read in a kind of jungle-chant, which seems appropriate given the little myth it conveys of royal intrigue and murder. You'll notice that she translates her own portmanteaus within the body of the poems.

Sudden Changing

```
   I kidly  ha  ha  ha  ha  ha  ha  ha  ha  ha
   ha  ha  ha  ha  ha   I killed loudly
  ja  ja  ja  ja  ja  ja  ja  ja  ja  ja  ja  ja  ja  ja
  ja  ja  ja  ja  A quebir  lo  lo  lo  lo  lo  lo  lo
   lo  lo  lo  lo  lo  lo  lo  lo  lo  lo  lo  lo  lo  lo
   lo  lo  lo  lo  lo  A queenbird   fe  fe  fe  fe  fe
   fe  fe  fe  fe  fe  fe  fe  fe  fe  fe  fe  fe  fe  fe
   fe  fe  fe  fe  fe  fe  fe  fe  fe  fe:  At nigoods
   ka  ka  ka  ka  ka  ka  ka  ka  ka  ka  ka  ka
   at night in the woods  fi  fi  fi  fi  fi  fi  fi  fi  fi
  fi  fi  fi  fi  fi  fi  fi  fi  fi  fi  fi  fi fi  fi  fi  fi  fi  fi
   fi  fi  fi  fi  fi  fi  fi  fi:  newnob I   ze     ze
  ze    ze              ze   ze       ze
     ze      ze:  nobody knew I    ta       ta
  ta      ta      ta      ta              ta
  turto a    bi   bi  bi  bi         bi  bi  bi    bi
  bi     bi           bi bi bi                  bi
     bi         bi bi   turned into a
   qu qu   qu      qu qu      qu qu      que
    qu qu    qu   a quebir      da  da  da
  da  da      da  da      da da      da  da
      da   da:  a queenbird    ne     ne
```

```
ne    ne    ne  ne    ne  ne
   ne   ne       ne    ne: by murdil.  Ti
 ti   ti      ti ti    ti ti        ti ti
   by murder.
```

—Ivanna

Quite as original and surprising at Liese's, this poem sneaks up on the reader (or the listener), inviting one into a jungle world where "dark things happen." What surprises me is how both poems can easily be traced to Lewis Carroll's original but are equally playful on their own.

Lesson 12: I Too Write with a Green Fish (A Bilingual Lesson)

Maybe Pablo Neruda was calling me—from his house by the edge of the dark rocks of the Pacific. He was calling me, wanting me to find again his voice. Years ago, I'd picked up his *Residence on Earth* in a Chicago bookstore in between buses, and on the long ride back to Ohio I'd been mesmerized by "Dead Gallop" and "Autumn Sonata" and "El Abandonado," as well as so many other of his equally dark and joyous poems. Now here I found myself on our first day in Chile driving through the maze of Santiago traffic and out onto the winding expressways to find his beach house at Isla Negra, which was turned into a resort in the last decade, but not so many years ago threatened by destruction at the hands of Pinochet's troops. I'd been invited to be a kind of poet-in-residence for an English-immersion school in Concepción several hours to the south, but for now we would spend some time wandering Neruda's ship-like home and playing on the rocks surrounding his beach. Standing there, I wondered how any of us could ever hope to replicate the intensity with which he lived his life. I'd been to several of Robert Frost's houses, with their New England austerity—and I could feel the energy of Frost's poems all around. It was the same here, except that this energy was new to me, full of stones and mastheads and bells and Neruda's great stuffed horse from childhood, set now in a mock stable at the entrance to the house. It was an exuberance Frost could hardly touch (though I love both of their poetries equally well).

In the gift shop, I bought several of his books and a poster and, reaching for the green pen to sign the slip, remembered what I'd just learned: that he wrote in green pen to better feel the energy of the earth. I wanted to tell the clerk that I, too, sometimes write in a green pen, but as she only spoke Spanish, I tried my best to get out a sentence: *Yo escribo también en un pez verde*, mistakenly calling up *pez*, which is "fish," to stand for *lápiz*, which means "pencil." How foolish. And yet I felt afterward that Neruda was again speaking through me. To write with a green fish might be to live again with the sea.

I told this story to one of the classes I met with in Chile—a sixth-grade classroom taught by Miss Jessica, who spoke no more English than I spoke Spanish. We'd planned the lesson together with the help of Julie Kessler, another teacher at the school, coming up with the idea that she would read "The Word" from Neruda's wonderful memoirs in Spanish first, and I would follow it in English. How lovely it all was. The students ran the bridge between us, speaking one language to me and another to their teacher—and writing their poems in both. When she read "The Word" in Spanish, they were intrigued; and for some reason, when I read the English translation, they spontaneously applauded.

We sat in a circle on the floor, took out pens and markers—and, inspired by Neruda's infectious love of words, on slips of colored construction paper wrote other words, in both languages. Sun and moon; *el sol y la luna*. Fish and sea; *la pez y el mar*. Shark and star; *el tiburón y la estrella*. Spanish on one side, English on the other. Then we let these words flutter to the floor between, landing on whichever side they would. Where they fell, we made new words: "The diamond bird," "the *cielo* chocolate" (the chocolate sky), *la oceano del oro* (the golden sea). Why had such a game not occurred to me before? Long ago I'd known that words had "rolled from sea to sea," the way Neruda describes, but to make it happen in our midst, as they fluttered together like blending leaves? It was too much fun to be believed. We just couldn't stop making combinations—and to do so, we had to decide which ones were just too obvious and which held more surprise, the "slinky dog" or the "sky of flowers"? The "moon man" or the "pizza of stars"? We were making words, I told them, the way Milton coined "pandemonium" from "all" and "demon" or the way "astronaut" was invented by linking "star" with "sailor." Why couldn't we do the same?

We listed these on the board . . . ah, but what next? Midway, I suddenly realized that the assignment I'd thought of doing did not fully match the exuberance and glory of their invented words. How, on the spot, to come up with something fresh? After conferring with Miss Jessica, stumbling around each other's languages, I remembered a poem by the Spanish poet José Luis Hidalgo, "Orilla de la Noche," the only poem I have memorized in both the original and its translation ("Shore of Night"), with its wonderful opening:

> ' Toda la noche de la tierra
> se me derrumba entre las manos . . .
> (All of the night on this earth
> is shattered between my hands . . .)

With the deep freedom of Spanish surrealism—the surrealism of Lorca, and the surrealism that Neruda, too, would make so much rich use of— I suggested that what Hidalgo could do, we too could do: imagine a world in which we could hold the night in our hands, in which the wonder of the planet could come alive, and *in which the words we had just invented could be real.* Through scrambling, it was "the right" assignment . . . or maybe Neruda conveyed through telepathy the assignment to us all? Being in Chile made me believe that such things could happen.

Poems from the Sixth Form of Thomas Jefferson School/Concepción, Chile:

> In the shine ocean
> was a moon man
> playing electric guitar.
>
> He was happy,
> he was free
> but when
> the diamond bird died
> he was so angry.
>
> He didn't feel good, he didn't want to do
> anything, because the bird is like his gold heart.
>
> —Emilio

> Estoy en el patio de mi casa, miro hacia arriba
> y veo un cielo de chocolate.
>
> Al verlo
> siento: alegría, hambre, ganas de subir
> hasta el cielo
>
> comerlo
> beberlo, tocarlo, saborearlo, tragarlo,
>
> bañarme en el,
> masticarlo, oberlo . . . cocinarlo . . .
>
> frevielo, mirarlo . . . desearlo tanto . . .
> . . . tenerlo . . . jugar con el . . .
> abrazarlo . . . mucho . . .
>
> dormir sobre el . . .
> soñarlo . . . me da tanta felicidad
>
> tener un cielo de chocolate . . .
>
> —Mario José

The Bright of the Night

The dark moon has a special bright.
Like a shine-ocean, but in the dark.
The dark mountain gave up, with the shadow sun.

But the darkness is falling over
and a flower sky woke up
to take the world to the brightness.

And the diamond bird flies in the sky
because the ocean tree is happy
and all the world is smiling.

But in the night, the darkness
covers the sun. And the star pizza,
and the dark arrives to the world.

—Victoria (6th grade)

Sueños

Nosotros podemos soñar
   muchas cosas soñar
Es cuando uno desea que su
   imaginación vuele
Por cielos de flores, brilliantes
   oceános, es cuando lo más
   raro

Hasta que salga el sol
Uno tiene tiempre de vivir
En una fantasía
Que lluevan flores, que
Nollon hombres en la luna
Que viajen y
conozcan soles de agua
pajaros de diamantes los aisles
vuelen por la luna
oscura
para darle
vida y brillo ellos
se ven en la noche
como estrellas brillando
en el cielo.

Dreams

We can dream anything

Dream is when imagination flies

In flower skies, shiny oceans,
is when these rare things can
  happen

Until the sun comes again
we have time to live
in a fantasy
where rain flowers and
there are men who walk on the moon
that travel and that
know water sun
diamond birds
that fly in the dark moon
for giving her
life and shine
They can be seen at night
like stars shining
in the sky.

—Anonymous (6th grade/
trans. by herself)

What more can I say? These were just the beginnings of learning to speak to each other. But I felt that these students, learning to become adept at two languages, were teaching the adults in the room (myself and Jessica) how to see with other eyes. Los ojos de poesía.

The Word

. . . You can say anything you want, yessir, but it's the words that sing, they soar and descend . . . I bow to them . . . I love them, I cling to them, I run them down, I bite into them, I melt them down . . . I love words so much . . . The unexpected ones . . . The ones I wait for greedily or stalk until, suddenly, they drop . . . Vowels I love . . . They glitter like colored stones, they leap like silver fish, they are foam, thread, metal, dew . . . I run after certain words . . . They are so beautiful that I want to fit them all into my poem . . . I catch them in mid-flight, as they buzz past, I trap them, clean them, peel them, I set myself in front of the dish, they have a crystalline texture to me, vibrant, ivory, vegetable, oily, like fruit, like algae, like agates, like olives . . . And then I stir them, I shake them, I let them go . . . I leave them in my poem like stalactites, like slivers of polished wood, like coals, pickings from a shipwreck, gifts from the waves . . . Everything exists in the word . . . An idea goes through a complete change because one word shifted its place, or because another settled down like a spoiled little thing inside a phrase that was not expecting her but obeys her . . . they have shadow, transparence, weight, feathers, hair, and everything they gathered from so much rolling down the river, from so much wandering from country to country, from being roots so long . . . They are very ancient and very new . . . They live in the bier, hidden away, and in the budding flower . . . What a great language I have, it's a fine language we inherited from the fierce conquistadors . . . They strode over the giant cordilleras, over the rugged Americas, hunting for potatoes, sausages, beans, black tobacco, gold, corn, fried eggs, with a voracious appetite not found in the world since then . . . They swallowed up everything, religions, pyramids, tribes, idolatries just like the ones they brought along in their huge sacks . . . Wherever they went, they razed the land . . . But words fell like pebbles out of the boots of the barbarians, out of their beards, their helmets, their horseshoes, luminous words that were left glittering here . . . our language. We came up losers . . . We came up winners . . . They carried off the gold and left us the gold . . . They carried everything off and left us everything . . . They left us the words.

—Pablo Neruda, from *Memoirs* (53–54)

----

5 Reflecting on Student Poems

Lesson 13: What Does Poetry Teach? Eight High School Writers

The Man Who Stole the Sun

I watched the man who stole the sun
I watched him fold it into his pocket
Wrapping it gently into a gift

I watched him walk carefully through
the darkness
I watched as only the street lamps
lit his way

> —Beth (10th grade/Fairbanks HS/
> Plain City, Ohio)

What does poetry teach? How does it let students speak about issues that are important to them? I wouldn't want the theory-based lessons described in this book to seem like a set formula, but rather establish a structure of conversation we might use to deepen our sense of what poetry does. Despite all the theories, it almost seems like each poem—whether by a student or a professional poet—offers a different answer. Much as the lessons we give students are often based on *techniques*, when students become adept at those, it is my belief that—just as with established poets—they will want to use those skills to speak about *what matters to them*. As an example, take Beth's poem, which sprang from an exercise based in Russell Edson's prose poetry, in which he often takes an "impossible" sentence (such as "A man with a huge eraser erases his daughter" or "We rowed upstairs in a canoe") and then plays out the possibilities if such a statement were true. It's a mythic way of viewing the universe, as Beth has here, playing with our sense of light and dark, of theft and gift, of vision and wonder. So maybe one thing that poetry teaches is how to recall our mythic beginnings, dipping our toe into the stream of consciousness and experience, and recalling that what is so ordinary around us is not quite so.

In the winter of 2000, I spent three months wandering the roads of Morrow, Marion, Delaware, and Union counties in central Ohio, visiting four different high schools for scattered periods of five days each as poet-in-residence for a project called Writing That Connects sponsored by the Ohio State University in Marion. Maybe it was the turn of the millennium that brought the poetry alive—but even though I'd been conducting such residencies for twenty years at that point, I heard their poems—and their need for poems—in a whole different way. Sometimes the lessons were born from dissatisfaction with what I'd already done—as in one small class after lunch at Fairbanks where I was not getting through to them and discarded the plan I'd brought to give them, which involved this one line by Lorca: "I want to sleep the dream of the apples." Without much discussion (they'd grown temporarily tired of discussing poems), I simply suggested they take his quiet, evocative line as a model and invent "impossible wants" of their own:

> I want to see
> With my ears
> I want to write
> With thoughts
> Eliminate the leaden middle man
> I want to know why
> For all the how, what, and where
> Which cannot be taught or read or spoken.
>
> —Neal (10th grade/Fairbanks HS/
> Plain City, Ohio)

So then, does poetry teach us how to live the impossible? To desire more than our daily lives can give? Does it express our dissatisfactions, whether we are in tenth grade or our fifth decade (I was fifty at the time)? Neal's poem has nary an image or metaphor in it—short of that marvelous central line about the "leaden middle man" of the pencil—but he's given voice to what poems are so often after: *speaking what we cannot say*.

I think that Amy, who is from another county, would agree, or would at least if she could speak in the voice of the following poem that was born from a quite different assignment, which was to make a list of words filled with alliteration, half-rhymes, and "the mutes" (strong emphasis on the letters *b, d, g, k, p, q,* and *t*) and then use at least two of them per line in a nonsense poem that at the same time gives advice:

How to Stay Sane

Pick the pines in the night
Tilt a dank, dark, dim pillow
Make a chuckle sound like thunder
Think on plains in November

Throw the moat around the gateway
Tear the tear upon the pathway

Keep a sense about you
Peel a tree, swing on fire

> —Amy (12th grade/Mt. Gilead HS/
> Mt. Gilead, Ohio)

Is it *sound* here that gives us meaning? Or is it sound that surrounds us until we can see fresh meaning? If language runs deep inside the nature of being human, as Lewis Thomas tells us in his *Lives of a Cell* (see following), maybe poetry opens up the words again, in unpredictable ways, new every time, as even lessons that we've taught before have to be reinvented each time we approach them.

Lewis Thomas on Language

"It begins to look, more and more disturbingly, as if the gift of language is the single human trait that marks us all genetically, setting us apart from all the rest of life. Language is, like nest-building or hive-making, the universal and biologically specific activity of human beings. We engage in it communally, compulsively, and automatically. We cannot be human without it; if we were to be separated from it our minds would die, as surely as bees lost from the hive."

> —*from "Social Talk"*
> (The Lives of a Cell, 105)

Poetry invites conversation, as Amy's poem does, imagining a listener out there who might be struck by her surreal advice. As does Justin's poem below, which seems to be addressed to someone in a distant memory—or maybe to himself:

Changes

Run . . .
I told you to run.
You stayed like an unmovable rock.
I knew it would happen,
They captured you and ran off.
Now our fun was crushed and stilled,
I told you to run,
Run . . .

> I come back and you're all grown up
> You changed more than I thought
> You're someone else, unfamiliar,
> Someone I never knew.
> I wish you would change,
> Or remember.
> > —Justin (12th grade/Elgin HS/
> > Elgin, Ohio)

Here Justin has taken his memory and made it into drama. Is *that* what poetry does? Let us relive our lives? Justin stood on the edge of his future when he composed this and, again, I can't help wondering if he saw himself in the past—or someone important to him back there—calling to him through the poem to *remember,* just as Stephanie does in her poem called "At the Stars":

At the Stars

> I remember the night you ignored
> The stars
> Deciding to deny the dancing
> Marvels
> Will an embrace release you to
> Map your soul?
> The night welcomes change
> Chase down yourself, and save me
> A part
> > —Stephanie
> > (12th grade/Mt. Gilead HS)

Stephanie and Justin could be talking to each other, even though they come from different schools. It seems that for both students poetry allows them to call back to parts of themselves—or, again, to others in their pasts—that might slip over the edge and be lost, as they themselves move on into adulthood. Their lines are simple, much more so than their essays on Poe or Hawthorne, or the equations they'd surely been doing in calculus or physics the period before. Yet their lines are as intricately woven as equations, filled with existential understanding, and built from delicate shifts in tone, as if on trellises of their souls.

Michael, in the following poem, seems to be saying the same thing, only this time it is based in more physical observation, as he looks at an old bell that has lost its clapper:

A Lost Heart (the Story of a Bell)

> Like the sound of a leprechaun tapping
> a pot of gold with his cane
> Such a small noise
> as the tap of a pencil would be

this wire, this clapperless wire
straining like a slave on his last hour
of sun, it tries to sound
but only little clinks come
out, sounding like the second hand
on a pocket watch No one acknowledged
its use, this bell so much like
us without a heart

    —Michael (10th grade/Mt. Gilead HS)

Sometimes it takes just such *observations of the small* to evoke such insight. And I'm surprised, looking back, at how Michael is able to evade tenth-grade masculine strictures against referring to something as sentimental as the heart in his poem. But he does, and he makes both the bell and our lives take on more meaning. As I've been saying throughout this book, dividing our visual/physical observations and experiences from our mental and inventive ones is nearly impossible, at least if we are to enter freshly the realm of poetry.

Here are two more new assignments—and I bring up all these poems merely to suggest how many options there are. Both ideas were born out of the desire to not-do-the-same-thing-again-at-least-not-in-quite-the-same-way. The first popped up unexpectedly on a day when I brought in one of my own poems, one in which I had been researching a poem on the Vietnam war, written for a dancer friend of mine whose father spoke of the "strafing songs" he and his buddies would play as they rode shotgun in their helicopters, strafing the jungle with random, desperate rounds of bullets. I gave this closing section:

The rounds disappear
like minnows below the paddies
cases of them
like voice in the bars
like rain across water
if rain could move with a beat
beyond forgetting
if the husks of rice could explode, empty,
could open and swallow hunger
like hunger
like buffalo into mist
like friends at home, like letters missed
that didn't come were never sent
like little scattering graves for thoughts
the gray rattling grave of thoughts
like VC dancers in their black pajamas
springing up or over a wall
like skimming the flipping fans of green

like notes on a rootless scale
riveting the forests the rivers the huts
the mountains the bunkers the valleys the paddies
like drowned pianos under the paddies
like riddles turning
like random periods tacking down sentences
that were never said
strung patterns of targets flopping & rising
like the spit of lies
the random spit of lies
the rattling alphabet spit of lies

—Terry Hermsen from "Strafing Songs"

Without using the poem to discuss too much of the horrors and disagreements of that war, I mainly wanted them to see that poetry could deal with all sorts of issues, from the personal to the political—and back again. And that even here, metaphor—and playing with form—became a way, and perhaps the only way, to deal with an experience most of us can only imagine.

So I suggested that they borrow the technique—stringing "likes" in a free associational sequence, which I myself might have unconsciously borrowed from a lesson I'd read about in a *Teachers & Writers* newsletter years ago, letting the lines themselves (and the surprises therein) guide where the poem might take them:

Like the tired dust flying from the piano strings
Like the new skin from a wound, tender and pink
Like the wailing silence of the grave
Like the saddest song
Like the sweetest smelling memory
Like the biting of your tongue as to not cut
Your own throat
Like the waltz preventing the stepping on toes
Like the Jack in the Box, tired of the song
Like the intimidation of the second hand as it moves
Like the wisdom of Father Time, clockwise
Like the simile comparing the opposite

—David (12th grade/Elgin HS)

I love how David's poem takes on its own territory—and finds ways to take even the most well-known of items (such as the jack-in-the-box) to invest with new energy. So the waltz is here to prevent the stepping on toes? Who would have thought? I can't help noticing how the form allows him to shift between concrete imagery and abstract allusions.

This last "poet" is really a whole class of writers, a group of tenth graders at Hayes High School in Delaware, Ohio. We had gathered in

the space of the auditorium stage one afternoon for a double period—
and it was that extra period that allowed for the richest exploration of
the week. We spent the first part of our time looking at the smallest of
poems, proverbs, and riddles, such as this Japanese proverb, translated
here by the poet W. S. Merwin, "Knows his way/stops seeing." By ex-
ploring the ways that even these ancient and tiny poem-mysteries con-
vey thought, we could then move to a more contemporary explorer of
such material, the visual artist Jenny Holzer, who grew up in Lancaster,
Ohio, only an hour or so away from their school, and who has gone on
to shake the art world with her introduction of verbal play on neon signs,
billboards, and ordinary sheets of typing attached to lampposts and city
walls. Phrases such as:

> ABUSE OF POWER COMES AS NO SURPRISE
>
> AN ELITE IS INEVITABLE
>
> PROTECT ME FROM WHAT I WANT
>
> MEN WON'T PROTECT YOU ANYMORE
>
> YOU ARE TRAPPED ON EARTH SO YOU WILL EXPLODE

With these examples in mind, we spread out around the stage and the
auditorium to write our own. We called them:

Jenny Holzerisms

When the world turns its back on you
anything is everything

*

Make your reflection who you are
not who you want to be

*

Let them fight—they will learn

*

Age is a byproduct of splendor

*

If you fall down once, get up
If you fall down twice, just lay there

*

The bubble always pops above a canyon

*

Swimming upstream will make you stronger
Going with the current you'll be washed away

*

Just because you don't know a language
doesn't mean that it's dead

        *

Our beds are cold when we have to get into them,
and warm when we must get out

        *

Glamour is a defense strategy

        *

You can't look personality in the eye
or tell it "no!"

        *

The one you stand up for is not always sitting

        *

What you do not miss you cannot love

        *

The ones who don't answer aren't always stupid

        *

The cheese should no longer have to stand alone

        *

Indifference can lead to extinction

        *

The man of many feelings is only wearing
what you're not

        *

Scales cover silences

        *

Scared—he puts on a uniform

        *

A person unseen is easy to find

        *

A smile isn't always a smile, until you know it is

        —Tenth-grade English class/
        Hayes High School/Delaware, Ohio

I will say little now, except to note that we wrote these out on cards and construction paper to paste around the school. Only signs announcing sporting events were allowed on school walls, so ours were removed by the next day. But we had our say—we'd made thought come alive, in the most condensed of language. *And maybe that's ultimately what poetry teaches.* All of the theories laid out in this book are just that—theories to predict and shape poems and lesson plans—but in the end, the poem still emerges from one writer sitting down with a blank sheet of paper and seeing "what can be done with words."

6 Reengaging the World

Lesson 14: Field Trip Ideas

Nearly every residency I've ever done, from city to rural to suburban schools, has included some sort of culminating poetry-writing field trip, testing out and applying what we've learned on excursions "out into the world." Several of these ideas are developed in detail in some of the lessons in Part II. The classes I worked with spent two days exploring different places around Mt. Gilead, Ohio, the town where many of the students grew up and which—until we went out and wrote in the state park, the downtown streets, and the local grocery—many of them reported never actually having really *seen* before. As one Mt. Gilead student said afterwards, "Why would I sit down on a park bench and spend time looking at the town? I live here. And most of the time we're just on our way to the movie, the store, the library. . . . I'd have no reason to." Yet that's precisely what writing poetry asks us to do: notice what we wouldn't notice. Lewis McAdams, in the early days of poetry-in-the-schools in this country, called poetry "the practice of outside. . . ." Taking those words seriously, I—and so many other poets across the land—have striven to do just that.

Here is an annotated list of various places I have taken students, on one-hour or all-day field trips, with some brief descriptions of possible slants for applying the skills of metaphor, physicality, visualization, and play we've been talking about all along.

1. Taking a Visit to the Science Fair

Two Quotes on Poetry, Science, and Knowledge

Unless you are at home in the metaphor, unless you've had your proper poetical education in the metaphor, you are not safe anywhere. You are not safe in science, you are not safe in history, *because you don't know the metaphor in its strengths and its weaknesses; you don't know how far you may expect to ride it and when it may break down with you.* (39)

—Robert Frost, "Education by Poetry"
(emphasis mine)

Poetry is an instrument of knowledge. (xvii)
   —Brewster Ghiselin,
   "Foreward" to *Modern Poetry of Western America*

I've always loved science fairs. You can find such nuggets of facts in them. Lightning strikes the earth 100 times a second. If you could weigh all the ants in the world, they would weigh more than all the mammals, fish, birds, and reptiles put together—four times over! And 1.2 million Earths could fit into the sun. This is wonderful stuff for poets—science that we can hold in our heads.

So when I arrived at Richwood Middle School one morning and noticed that a science fair had taken over the gym downstairs, I threw out my plans immediately and improvised a little tour, asking students to walk around, jot down at least five interesting facts they discovered, and then to bring those facts back to the classroom. The wonderful Ohio-born poet Mary Oliver once said: "I like to have plenty of facts in my poem, because then I can dream around them" (comment made in class at The Ohio State University, fall 1983). I showed the students Oliver's "Snakes in Winter" (see following poem) and suggested the following options for weaving their own dreams-of-the-world:

a. Pretend you're having a dream of this subject (volcanoes or clouds, etc.) and include in subtle ways the facts, not as a list, but as an interior part of your poem. Show us what you know about the subject by applying it.

b. *Become* the subject . . . as in Jayne's "Tropism" poem. Again, include the facts in ways that make them seem natural to your poem.

c. Write an *ode* to your subject . . . as in Pablo Neruda's "Ode to Salt" (see Robert Bly's anthology *News of the Universe*). Like Neruda, *exaggerate* your subject, illuminating its subtle wonders through metaphors that change how we see.

Snakes in Winter

Deep in the woods,
under the sprawled upheavals of
    rocks,

dozens lie coiled together.
Touch them: they scarcely

breathe; they stare
out of such deep forgetfulness

that their eyes are like jewels—
and asleep, though they cannot
    close.

And in each mouth the forked
    tongue,
sensitive as an angel's ear,

lies like a drugged muscle.
With the fires of spring they will
    lash forth again

on their life of ribs!—
bodies like whips!

But now under the lids of their
    mute
succeeding snowfalls

they sleep in their cold cauldron: a
    flickering broth
six months below simmer.

—Mary Oliver

Tropism

As I sit in my pot,
No light, I will die.

So I turn.
I turn for my life.

It is so hard.

But I make it.
Just in time.

—Jayne (5th grade/North Union
Elementary/Richwood, Ohio)

2. In the Science Room

Other spaces around the school can take on new energy when used for the purposes of poetry. Sometimes I've asked a science teacher with a great collection of "stuff" in his or her laboratory (skulls, snakes, shells, mollusks, fish, models of the universe) if we could switch rooms for the day, then offered the student poets I'm working with a chance to visualize the wonders of science with new eyes. One game we've played is the following: moving from station to station to gather observations, metaphors, and possibilities, then we read some contemporary poems based in the poetics of science (I suggest Mark Brown's wonderful anthology *Verse and Universe* as a source) and try our own.

Poetry in the Science Room: A Game

STARTERS: Everyone chooses a "station"—a case, a spot in the room. Your first lines will begin from that location, following the directions that come next.

A.   Write some lines (not thinking of a full poem yet) in response to what you observe.

    1.   Begin with two incomplete sentences.
    2.   Follow with an outlandish comparison or metaphor.
    3.   Refer to something <u>not</u> in the room using one or more of your senses.
    4.   Return to the object in front of you—only now it has shifted somehow, as if in a dream.

B.   At this point, turn to face the rest of the room and choose some object or case most nearly "opposite" from what you've just been writing about.

    5.   Begin a line with "I thought . . ."
    6.   Write a line (or a couple of lines) using two of the senses.
    7.   Repeat—nearly—something you said earlier, but shift it somehow.
    8.   Mix something from your home or your own life with the object before you.

C.   Count two "spaces" to the right.

    9.   Make a list of five nouns and five verbs.
   10.   Then write four or five lines that use those nouns and verbs in unexpected ways.

D.   At this point, silently go to the window, or step out into the hall. Write a series of three to four lines that somehow continue what you were writing above.

E.   Return to the object you were writing about under "B".

   11.   Write a line that begins "Now" or "I always" or "Whenever".
   12.   Write a line that refers to something someone once told you.

F.   Move to a spot two or so "spaces" to the left.

   13.   Have this creature or object do something it wouldn't normally do.
   14.   Write a line in future tense, so that part of the poem begins to sound like a prediction.
   15.   Close the poem with a strong image (a line or lines that create a picture in our minds), which somehow refers to something you said earlier.

G.   Take some time—either now or overnight—to cut, revise, juggle what you've got here as rough notes into a fuller poem.

Two Student Poems

Audience

When he was frightened to death
Scared into the stiffness of the walls
His eyes, piercing, pink, like
    strawberry candy
Remind me of crisp, fallen leaves that
never crunched loudly
beneath his careful feet
He vanishes into the clouds, only
    his pink eyes remain.

I thought he was part of a collection
    of frozen heads
The buffalo with a beard of wires
And a scent, not like death, but not
    of living
I thought he was frozen, his eyes
    closed
Finally at peace with all his sur-
    roundings

His hours are racing to the heavens
His eyes showing there was once a
    soul
White bands of fur strangling his
    neck
Alert ears waiting for someone to
    wake him
While his nose stares out at me, his
singular audience.

—Allison
Elgin High School

Under the Clock

Under the clock
Next to the chalkboard
A box of dead beauty steals the
Eye of attention as a piercing
Thief
The tree rustling in the wind can
Only break the silent barrier of
Concentration
The countless numbers of bugs
    engross
My body, my mind
I thought plants didn't know how
    to fly
Sitting next to them makes me free
Cooling breeze touches my face,
    the gentle
Sound of the wind sweeping under
    the
Wings fill my mind with wonders
    of
Coarse grass and scattered clouds
My mind is here, forever lost in
    thought, until
The tree shifts to once again
    become comfortable
The imitation of the plastic Lepi-
    doptera can
Never compare to the unique
    sculpting
Of its fragile wings
The omniscient feather observes
    the world
The intense eye communicates
    with its
Insomnia
The aware tree perches itself on the
Earth, unknown creatures yet to
    form

—Sarah
Elgin High School

3. The Furnace Room

There are often plenty of other overlooked spaces for poets to wander in practically any school. One place I've found inviting, if there's enough space to not interfere with the machines, is the furnace room. How often do we consider this little dungeon below our feet, this place of heat and steam, sound and texture? With the custodian's permission—and sometimes with his or her explanation for "what is going on"—I've spent numerous hours helping students find poetry in what is (literally and invisibly) right below their feet.

4. The Life of a Factory

Factories also are wonderful places for gathering intriguing physical imagery. Among others, I've taken kids to a boat factory and a washing-machine plant. A friend of mine got great poems from taking students to a local slaughterhouse. Many factories will set up tours if you ask, and some already give their own. I love taking a day to do some preliminary writing in the morning, going on an extended tour of a local factory, and then finding a place to write poems based on our observations. I just ask that the tour guide give us three or four spots of a few minutes each to record what we're seeing and hearing. I will give the students worksheets divided into columns labeled "Facts"/"Observation and Detail"/and "Metaphor," which give them plenty to go on when we sit down to write poems at the end.

There are many fine model poems that stem from work experiences—Gary Snyder's "Mid-August at Sourdough Mountain Lookout," or "Hay for the Horses," for instance, or his poems about working on oil tankers. There also are Philip Levine's or Jim Daniels's poems about working in the auto industry. And then there's the wonderful anthology, *Working Classics*, with so many angles on factory life. Read a few of these with your students, and then ask them to take one of the following approaches:

a. Pretend to be one of the workers here, describing your day in poem form. Be careful not to whine or easily lament "the hard work"—rather, make it real—using metaphor and detail to help us visualize the tasks and the feelings.

b. Again, make use of dream to give a sense of the "other realities" here, but using the facts and details to ground that dream in the location. As with the first option, it would be easy enough to create a Chaplin-like machine nightmare. Avoid that. Find your own slant to what "the dream of the factory" would be like.

c. Take ALL of your details and facts, metaphors, and observations and weave them into a kind of loose "tour of the factory" in distinctive phrases and images—making use of the whole page—letting the lines take on their own units and spacing. Your poem could be a kind of "word map" of all you saw, etched with textures and nuance.

5. Restored Theaters

An old theater, especially one that's been restored, can be a fine place to spark our dreams. Even when nothing's going on, the seats and the ceiling, the stage and the screen can spring alive and suggest a drift in time quite conducive to poetry. With one high school class, we took a tour of the Ohio Theater in downtown Columbus and had a magnificent time, taking "the notes of a poet" all along the way. We were taken back stage, experienced the lighting options, heard the story of the restoration—and of the mythical characters embedded high above our cinematic eyes. Then we got permission to spread out, each finding a seat far away from others, and wrote our poems-of-the-movies. There are some fine examples in the anthology *Lights, Camera, Poetry*. Movies are so much a part of our world, there must be a hundred ways that poets can reflect on these urban caverns of the soul.

6. The Art Museum

There is, of course, a centuries-old tradition of poets visiting museums to write ekphrastic poems in response to the artwork. Why not take a morning—or a whole day—getting a tour of a nearby museum and then spreading out around the galleries to write? My experience has been that after a week or so of gathering the skills outlined in the exercises of this book, any class is ready to try their hand at writing from paintings and sculpture, as visually evocative and inviting-of-metaphor as good artwork often is.

My suggestion is to look at a few examples first. There are many, but three of the ones I keep coming back to as models are:

- William Carlos Williams's "Pictures from Bruegel" sequence, especially "Self Portrait" and "Hunters in the Snow." These offer fine models for writing without punctuation, treating the lines on the page as a way to build a portrait in words.
- Wislawa Szymborska's "Bruegel's Two Monkeys" (see p. 174) with its evocative blend of detail and invention.

- Lawrence Raab's "An Old Photographer from Vermont" (see p. 124), which is excellent for working with portraits.

I mention a number of such approaches in Lessons 1 and 7 in Part I, and Lessons 28 and 29 in Part II, but one other useful setup is to suggest that the students choose one of three approaches—or try a different approach in three different galleries:

a. Write *from* the painting—as if you were someone or something inside the artwork. If you've done previous work with oppositions or persona, students should be able to step right into this idea.

b. Write *to* someone or something in the artwork—in a kind of open-eyed ode . . . wondering about them . . . talking to them. . . .

c. Write *about* the artwork, describing it with as careful an eye as possible, as W. C. Williams does. Through metaphor, color, gesture, surprise, and point-of-view, your job is to bring the artwork alive in words.

Sometimes I have used the technique of doing "alphabet circles" for taking notes in front of a painting, writing the letters of the alphabet in a circle around the page, such as:

Students then find words that relate to the painting for as many of these letters as they can—though never feeling they have to fill them all in, nor that they can't have more than one word for each letter. The idea is much more to develop an expansive vocabulary for speaking about the work—as well as to lengthen their attention span, allowing the textures of the painting to soak in, rather than dashing off a poem too quickly.

Here's an example of a poem written from a painting in the Columbus Museum of Art using this method:

> **Air, Iron, Water   (Robert Delauney, 1936)**
>
> Sun shatters
> As if a breath could break
> Into a dozen tunnels—
> Like puzzles strung together
>
> Into loops and lace.
> Where is the shelter?
> It rides inside each bubble,
> Bursting across the green shadow,
>
> Spun into atoms
> And arches and angles.
> Board then the train
> To this new time.
>
> Each arrow you follow
> Will point you everywhere.
>
> —Terry Hermsen

7. The Historical Society

Most towns of any size—and certainly most good-sized cities—have historical societies just waiting for visitors. I've taken students to museums as small as Marion's "Popcorn Museum" and as large as Columbus's "Ohio Historical Society," with its massive reconstructed town from the 1890s. As with the previous examples, the "game" here is to wander with a poet's eyes, gathering facts, making detailed observations, even doing interviews with storekeepers or docents, and then finding a place to block out all the distractions and *write*. Become one of the people in the past (as Margaret Atwood does in "The Planters," her poem about Susanna Moodie, a woman who moved to the Canadian wilderness in the 1840s), or in the voice of one of the "objects of history" so prevalent in museums (as Herman Melville does in his Civil War-era poem, "On an Uninscribed Monument at One of the Battlefields of the Wilderness"). Persona in poetry allows us to take so many directions. It's a way of making your poems physical and visionary at once.

8. Downtown Streets

Gertrude Stein used to park her car near a busy Paris intersection and just write about all that circled so frantically around her, thus breaking the image of the lonely poet retreating to his or her attic "to be alone." It can be stimulating to wander the streets of any town or city. I cover in more detail some options in Lessons 23 through 26 in Part II, but all these can be expanded and adapted to nearly anywhere. If there is lots of activity on the street (say at lunch hour), it's fun to sit on park benches and make up little biographies, the way the English novelist H. E. Bates is said to have done, sketching out potential childhoods, fears, loves, secrets, memories—and writing portrait poems. Writers are explorers of the world, as well as their own minds. Why not let your class do the same? Some model poems to build some city lessons around are:

a. Frank O'Hara's "The Day Lady Died" or "A Step Away from Them"

b. Denise Levertov's "Blue Africa"

c. Osip Mandelstam's "Leningrad" or "Mandelstam Street"

d. William Carlos Williams's "Between Walls" or "Proletarian Portrait"

e. Carl Sandburg's "Night"—or many of his Chicago poems

f. Gwendolyn Brooks's "We Real Cool"

Writing poems about the streets where we live can make the daily life of our surroundings swarm with new meaning. Students don't only need "lessons" in poetry—or history or science—they need experiences to help them believe this world is worth living in.

9. Caves

Caves also are often intriguing places to explore with poetry. For if, as Flannery O'Connor says, "It is the business of [art] to embody mystery," isn't there something of a deep mystery to these underground rooms of stone? Again, I've come to feel that with enough interest and training in poetry, such an adventure nearly writes itself. Choose some poems that evoke the natural world—or a sense of inside and outside, or the mix of real world knowledge with surreal possibilities, such as Howard Nelson's "Cows Near the Graveyard," Mary Oliver's "Sleeping in the Forest," or Elizabeth Bishop's "Sleeping on the Ceiling"—and let the ideas grow from there. This might be a point where you can build the options for the writing assignment *together* with your students, reading the example poems first and then assigning them in pairs the task of coming up with at least two writing ideas to offer to the group. You might be surprised by how much they've absorbed over the course of your poetry writing in shaping their own ideas for how to approach a poem in a particularly evocative place like this one.

10. The Zoo

The zoo is another location available to many communities. While listing all the ideas for writing that could be tackled in a visit would require a book in itself, the basic idea would be to build an atmosphere of inquiry into the day, guiding the students in ways that go beyond the usual running-from-cage-to-cage that characterizes many visits to the zoo. On one field trip, we found an out-of-the-way spot to set up our tour, looking at some example poems first and noting how much close attention went into these diverse styles:

- Mary Oliver's "Snakes in Winter" (or any number of her other fine animal-observation poems)
- Wallace Stevens's existential "A Rabbit as King of the Ghosts"
- Harley Elliott's "Whales" or "Ants"
- William Blake's "The Tyger"
- Pattiann Rogers's "Elegy for A Hermit Crab"

Then set up an assignment in which students closely observe and take notes on at least three of the zoo's creatures, writing poems in several different styles—a dream poem for or about that animal; a close description of the animal, using all your poetic skills; an ode to the animal; and, of course, a persona poem in the voice of that animal.

In distracting environments like this one, I always tell the students: pretend it's perfectly normal to be sitting here taking notes and writing a poem as the crowds mill by. Yours is just a different kind of concentration, halfway between a scientist's and a dreamer's.

Lesson 15: Bantu Combinations: An Exercise in Drinking in the World

You have read everything
but drunk nothing
       —surrealist proverb

This is an exercise in "drinking in the world," one that can be done anywhere—in the woods, on the playground, in a city park, or even in the classroom. It starts with considering the "roots of lyric," Andrew Welsh's phrase for the deep historical sources of the lyric poem, which he says spring out of tribal traditions from nearly all cultures of the world in the area of proverbs, charms, and riddles (see Lessons 4 and 13).

You can, for instance, see that same kind of "inner potability" in nearly any good *ghazal*, as in this opening couplet from "August 1952" by Faiz Ahmed Faiz:

> It's still distant, but there are hints of springtime:
> Some flowers, aching to bloom, have torn open their collars.

Or these ending lines from "The Blackberry Thicket" by Ann Stanford, which I've quoted elsewhere:

> Surely not alone
> I stand in this quiet in the shadow
> Under a roof of bees.

Poems like these grow out of the lyric sensibility to take in the world, present in all cultures across time. Here's a slightly different form from the Bantu, but one equally rooted in energetic language, a kind of call-and-response poem using paired lines and stressing "off-hand" connections:

Bantu Combinations:

1.
I am still carving an ironwood stick.
I am still thinking about it.

2.
The lake dries up at the edges.
The elephant is killed by a small arrow.

3.
The little hut falls down.
Tomorrow, debts.

4.
The sound of a cracked elephant tusk.
The anger of a hungry man.

5.
Is there someone on the shore?
The crab has caught me by one finger.

6.
We are the fire which burns the country.
The Calf of the Elephant is exposed on the plain.

It's fun to talk about the combinations here—how they speak indirectly to each other. At the same time, it's also possible to "let them stand," hearing the combinations as if they were parts of song lyrics. Either way, tapping into these poems, along with some riddles, is a good setup for tackling the following exercise:

Bantu Combinations* . . . a group exercise/experiment:

Step 1:

1. Groups of twelve to twenty-four form a circle, each person facing *outward*.

2. Count off and number your paper accordingly, leaving a second line or space after each numbered line.

3. Write *one line* in the space corresponding to your number, drawing on inspiration from the territory that surrounds you (making use of sharp description, surprising metaphor, compressed imagery, wicked irony . . . as you will)

4. Then starting with 1, each person reads out what he or she has written—loud enough for all to hear—but with all of us still facing outward.

5. Each of us "responds" to that line, writing that second line in the space on your paper that corresponds to that writer's number.

6. The trick, of course, is to respond appropriately—but offhandedly—leaping to a connection that at first might not even seem clear to you but that might form some tangential or ironic connection.

7. Continue around the circle, each person reading out their first line, with everyone responding, until all lines have been covered.

Step 2:

Reading back:

8. First, still facing outward, go back to the first person, but this time as the line is read, someone "answers" from the line they wrote in response. In fact, several people might choose to answer.

9. Continue around, reading from one to three responses for each first line.

---

* This game has gone through several variations, but the original one was invented by Stuart Lishan and myself at an arts camp for gifted students at The Ohio State University in the summer of 1995.

10. Star any answer that you read back, just so we can re-create the reading when all the groups get back together.

Step 3:

11. Reshaping the poems . . . An exercise in instant revision: pair up and think of all the answers that both of you made as raw material for a poem. Choosing between them—and even cutting or editing—construct a poem from your lines that in some way fits together . . . *connecting* responses in off-hand, intriguing ways.

Lesson 16: How to Do a Poetry Night Hike

From ancient times, the night has been for stories, and myths spun from embers or stars, well before the blue of the TV screen. Here's one: I am doing a poetry residency at Cloverleaf Junior High School, a gray-brown, featureless, moderately new building set in the midst of north-central Ohio farmland. One evening after a long day at school, Jann Gallagher, a CJHS English teacher, takes me for a tour of the school's land lab, a wooded area sloping down to a small creek and its steep embankment, all wonderfully restful after the crowded halls, all within a literal stone's throw from a major four-lane truck route. On the way back, walking through the upper meadow, I let slip the words, "Hey, we could do a poetry night hike here. . . ."

Little did I know what a *poetry* night hike was. My first wife, Carla, had conducted several environmental night hikes at outdoor education camps in Ohio, though I'd never gone on one. But I underestimated the person I was speaking with—an energetic teacher always looking for a way to spark her students' love of language and the world, and the only member of the faculty here (I found out later) to make consistent use of the land lab with her classes. Within three days, she'd arranged the hike, talked three teachers and nearly twenty-five students, along with her own nine-year-old daughter, into participating, and we were set for the following Wednesday. But what exactly were we going to do?

At least I had the weekend to think about it. If writing residencies were really a place for experimentation, and if poetry was to meet these kids' lives outside the desk-bound classroom, here was a chance to prove it. On the long drive home I began composing ideas.

Years, and several such excursions later—including night hikes in Vermont, California, and two Ohio state parks—here's what I think a poetry night hike can be: a cross between the fourteenth-century Japanese tradition of writing group *renga* (in which participants build a long poem together over the course of an evening) and a typical American outdoor education camp's Thursday evening activity in which students explore the mysteries of the unlit half of the world. I believe poetry night hikes are most of all a blend of silence and words. Using that creative opposition, it's up to the planners to structure an event that mixes those two elements in interactive ways. On the language side, one might include some writing of poems—individually or as a group, on paper or out loud—along with the reciting or reading of poems by one or more members, with the others gathered around in the darkness, testing how the twists of the words find their way up through the pines like quickly vanishing smoke. However, these verbal projections can be alternated with plenty of receptive time, such as walks done in silence, owl calls, the gathering of objects, and games for awakening our often brittle (because unused) night senses, particularly touch and hearing. Whatever mix is chosen, any "plan" will of course be adjusted to the nature of the group and the terrain to be covered. The progression should be slow, gradually letting the senses open wider, the way the rods in our eyes find their own way of gathering in the light. Each hike is different, even in the same terrain. The feel of the night at hand should influence the outline. The idea is not to follow any set formula. Rather, it is to find spaces within earth's "dark skirts" as Mary Oliver puts it, to listen.

On that first hike, we improvised. At early dusk, we gathered in that same meadow on the hillside above the school woods. From a song by John Denver (which one of the kids' families I was staying with was playing in their home the week before) with the lines "Some days are diamonds, some days are stones," I created an exercise in which each participant contributes a line beginning with "Some nights are . . . ," followed with a metaphor. "Some nights are hollow secrets / Some nights are suspended webs. . . ." Not exactly new lyrics for the radio, but hints of what we might find down there in the woods. (Are all poems a kind of preparation?) Next, we walked in a line down the small slope, forming a group "caterpillar": placing our hands on the shoulders of the one in front of us, we closed our eyes, all except the leader, who led us down the hill any way but straight. Giggles. Twists. Stumbles. Holding on, tripping on each other's shoes, we came down into the now much-darker forest. Had our eyes adjusted so quickly? We broke into small groups—and with the aid of two teachers trained in outdoor education techniques, we investigated the small areas around us, "washing our hands in the leaves" and matching the shapes of those on the ground with the ones still in the trees.

Later, at a small amphitheater of seats down by the creek, the students listened while I recited a few poems about the night. In my planning, I'd been surprised by how many of the poems I'd memorized over the years had to do with night, including William Stafford's "Traveling through the Dark," Mary Oliver's "Sleeping in the Forest," Robert Frost's "Acquainted with the Night," and the Spanish poet José Luis Hidalgo's "Shore of Night" (see Lesson 10), among others. What is it about night that draws poets to it? Perhaps it is the heightened sense that just as in a poem, there are yet to be uncovered layers, as Robert Bly says, "waves breaking on shores / just over the hill." Like language, night is there and present every day of our lives; a polar presence to our claims of mastery and understanding, and yet we are often so removed from it. The poem hopes to bring us closer.

Listen to these stanzas:

> All of the night on this earth
> is running out between my hands
> like water trying to run away
> between bulrushes and birds.
>
>   —José Luis Hidalgo, "Shore of Night"

> Whatever it was I lost, whatever I wept for
> Was a wild, gentle thing, the small dark eyes
> Loving me in secret.
>
>   —James Wright, "Milkweed"

> I thought the earth
> remembered me, she
> took me back so tenderly, arranging
> her dark skirts, her pockets
> full of lichens and seeds.
>
>   —Mary Oliver, "Sleeping in the Forest"

> The car aimed ahead its lowered parking lights;
> under the hood purred the steady engine.
> I stood in the glare of the warm exhaust turning red;
> Around our group I could hear the wilderness listen.
>
>   —William Stafford, "Traveling Through the Dark"

Quietly, then, we moved up the last trail toward the school. I'd asked the group to remain in full silence and explained that we would be doing what is known as a "Seton Watch" before we left the woods. For this, as we moved up the trail, participants would be tapped on the shoulder by the leader every ten feet or so and asked to sit in silence on the trail, simply paying attention to where they were, and listening and watching. Because we would be within ready reach of the group, we would be perfectly safe, but because we were far enough away so that we couldn't see anyone else, we would get a chance to feel what it's like to be "alone in the night." Would we be able to shut down the little voices of worries that run through our heads continually? I tried not to sound melodramatic here. It was a simple thing we would be doing: spending ten minutes watching one of the most basic phenomena on earth; the ritual passage from light to dark, as people across all cultures have done for millennia. And yet I knew the experience was odd to us, something we seem to remember only distantly.

Back at the room, we got—among others—this poem from Bill, a student then in seventh grade:

Trapped

Trapped,
In my brain.

Misty,
I see words floating
Around in my brain,
All school related
Words.
All of a sudden
The walls start
To close together,
As if they didn't
Want me.

A door
Flies open,
I jump out.
I keep falling,
Falling
Down,
Stairs all around
Until I almost
Hit bottom.
Then,
A truck roars by,
With its horn blasting.

Waking me out of a trance,
Until I am back
Under the tree
Gazing into the sky.

> —Bill (7th grade/Cloverleaf
> Junior High School/Lodi, Ohio)

Clearly this was no run-of-the-mill experience for Bill. (He'd told me on the way back up the hill of a sense that his mind really wanted to close up, wanted him gone. . . .) Notice, however, that it's not only the strange vision that counts in the end, but how the sky has cleared, and he's back under the tree, watching. There is nothing more that a night hike can hope to accomplish, if it helps one student see the world more clearly.

Many poetry night hikes have followed over the years, each one adapted to the particulars of their locations—a rich mountain meadow in northern California; along a rocky stream called Furnace Run in Cuyahoga National Park as part of a two-day retreat for seventh graders in Mohican State Park in Ohio. Sometimes we write inside afterwards, and sometimes out in the immediacy of the forest itself. Perhaps my favorite was in a meadow surrounded by Cooper's Woods for a group of ninth graders near Lodi, Ohio, where we gathered in a central circle to do an opening exercise. Then just at the edge of dusk, we all turned our backs to the circle we'd formed and stepped out along invisible spokes, seventy yards or more, to the point where our individual radius met with the edge of the woods, and then wrote poems (since they'd been studying mythology) as if the night were an oracle speaking to them secrets only poems can tell. Such as this one:

> I see softly something that day cannot bring.
> I hear sounds that touch deep inside me.
> The droplets of moonlight caress my face.
> The darkness I feel is that of many years gone by.
> Any sounds I hear are of a world
> I dare not travel.
> For in my world, the night, silence is
> just something to make up for the mistakes of sound.
> And sound just pushes silence
> further into my world.
> For when a bird flies he doesn't
> fly toward sound, he flies toward silence.
>
> —Missy (9th grade/Cloverleaf Junior High)

Choosing to close this half of the book with night-hike stories, I am aware that many schools and areas might not have a land lab right out their back door, but they may have a woods or metro park to which they can travel. I believe there are territories to explore anywhere, even in the daytime, which can help students engage with worlds outside their classroom enclosures. One poet friend of mine, Nancy Kangas, has taken the poetry night hike idea and applied it to residencies she has done *in the city, in the daytime,* guiding students on walks to explore their neighborhoods. In his Nobel Prize speech, Pablo Neruda said, "In the course of my life I have always found somewhere the necessary affirmation, the formula which lay waiting for me, not to be petrified in my words, but to explain me to myself" (17). If the ideas in this book hold any validity at all, they hover around how the skills of metaphor, physical exploration, visual imaging, and playfulness can help students, just as Neruda did and as Bill and Mindy do in the previous poems, explain themselves to themselves—wherever they live.

II The Mt. Gilead Project: A Semester with Poetry

7 Classroom Exercises

For the longest time, Mt. Gilead was just a stopping place for me on cross-state travels, as I avoided the expressway. I liked the little home-owned ice cream shop on the north side of town, and the way traffic took a jag around the monument at the town center. I *wanted* to imagine this town as a good place to live, the way I did with other towns across the state and the United States, having ridden my bike through so many and stopping for lunch, or just a soda, at the local diner, listening in on the talk of the regulars. But to actually *live* here—that would be another matter. Nearly thirty years ago (from 1978 to 1983), my first wife and I moved to a town something like this, in north Richland County, and tried hard to form connections, stopping in the bike shop to talk, pausing with a teller at the bank who admired our bright-eyed one-year-old daughter, and feeling hopeful when the owner of the local gas station asked to come over for a chat (turned out he wanted us to join his Amway team). In the end, we failed to make the life there we'd wanted. The teaching jobs were being cut back, not expanded. We got to know almost nobody.

In some ways I'd also remained a stranger in all the poetry residencies I'd had around the state for the past twenty-five years—in Shiloh, New Washington, Lodi, Westfield Center, Chatham, Apple Creek, Savannah, and Butler. One comes in as a guest—an unknown entity—bringing the exotic fruit of poetry. And one connects with a teacher or two, or a few of the students. But what is left behind? I began to wonder about more than that: who were these kids to begin with? What sort of place does a poet—or any artist from the outside—venture into when visiting a school or a small community? What would happen if we took the principles I'd been exploring somewhat randomly over the years and applied them more deliberately? I came back to Mt. Gilead to find out.

Through several teacher workshops and short residencies in her class, I knew that Jill Grubb was a teacher I'd love to collaborate with, so I asked her if she'd be willing to have me visit two of her tenth-grade English classes over the course of a semester. By deliberately, if fluidly, laying out a series of lessons connected to the theories I've discussed in Part I of this book, I wanted to see if we could connect poetry to more students. I was overjoyed at her acceptance and am forever grateful for her collaboration. All we discovered in what we began to call our "Mt.

Figure 7.1. Jill Grubb, "After the Poetry Reading"

Gilead Project"—an experiment dedicated to discovering ways in which poetry might help students rediscover the places where they live—is in large part due to the atmosphere she set up and her willingness to bring poetry into the whole of her curriculum (see Figure 7.1).

Lesson 17: Poetry and the Reengagement of Our Lives

I started out the first day with a little ice-breaking exercise; an activity that I thought would take fifteen minutes but expanded to more than an hour, for the students turned my questions into a chance to show off in front of each other, as well as to listen to each other's stories. On this day, they found out things about each other that many didn't know. What's more, they seemed to treasure that knowledge.

I asked them for three things, jotted down on index cards: (1) A story that someone had once told them—perhaps a grandparent or an uncle; (2) Something that they know how to do that maybe no one else in the room would; and (3) Some fact they've come across that interests them. I gave them examples of my own. For number 1, I told the story my dad told me, for instance, about choosing between three jobs when he graduated from college in 1949, and how he took the more stable—and less intriguing—offering mainly because he had a family to support, with one three-year-old son and another (namely me) on the way.

For number 2, I mentioned my ability to juggle, which I learned through careful demonstration by a former student of mine, who taught me to "take gravity out of it" in the beginning, by rolling the balls in the appropriate pattern on the floor. And for number 3, I gave them the odd statistic that an average-size cloud doesn't weigh "nothing," as many students guessed, but instead a whopping 550 tons (impossible . . . but true).

Through luck or intuition, I'd picked questions that they had a lot to say about. Almost all had little weird stories, from their parents' or their own lives; they all could do things that surprised the rest of us; and many carried odd little facts in their brains:

> —*Jenny* [for instance], whose mother once had a job in the pet department at a Wal-Mart in Minnesota and on her last day let all the birds out of their cages.

> —*Amber*, who can fly a plane . . . and knows that each aspirin takes one teaspoon of blood from your heart.

> —*Nate*, who was willing to admit that last year for Halloween he and his friends "painted up and dressed like cheerleaders."

> —*Ben V.*, who seemed fascinated with the idea that "if all the people in China stood in a line, it would never end," for there would always be someone being born to keep the line going.

Most of all, they loved the odd facts and confessions:

> —*Ci'Arra*, who tells us that it is impossible to lick your elbow—or that in your life you will swallow an average of eight spiders.

> —*Julie*, who admits that "when I was little, when I got mad, I'd bang my head on the floor . . . " and that "I can change a colostomy bag."

> —*Jordan*, who enjoys relating that when his grandfather was in high school "he was a greaser and had the fastest car in town b/c he figured out how to put 3 carburetors on the engine."

But I'm just as interested in the less flashy confessions:

> —*Ryan's* family runs a thriving family farm of 2,000 acres.

> —*Sarah M.* was born on Easter and writes: "Learning someone's religion is more important than where they're from" and that her mom was a missionary in the Philippines.

> —or that *Sarah S.* plays string bass in the Mansfield Youth Orchestra.

> —or that *David C.* knows that Canal Winchester, a town down near Columbus, has a large parade every year they call "The World Parade."

I like knowing that Sara G. remembers that cows have five compartments in their stomachs; or that Jenny has studied ant colonies that make slaves of other ants; or that Sarah K. knows the name for the little white spots above a horse's hooves ("socks"), that "blue eyes on horses are called 'glass eyes,'" and that she can neigh "and used to call [her] horse" that way.

Some were less willing to share (or had less to put down)—and, oddly enough, these usually proved to be the less involved writers as our time went on. Looking at the cards from four of the weakest writers from the whole experience, I see they are about one-third as full as most of the rest, with only the skimpiest of details. In fact, the entire information from the *sum total* of their combined four cards barely equals what other students wrote individually:

G.:
(1) When my mom was in labor with me, she went to Krogers and walked around to try and kill time.
(2) I play sports pretty well.
(3) [blank]

M.:
(1) My grandfather told me when his dad was in WWI, he killed someone and was never the same.
(2) whistle very loudly.
(3) [blank]

H.:
(1) My grandpa almost drowned when he was young and now he's scared of water.
(2) Cheerleading.
(3) [blank]

D.:
(1) I jumped off a bunk bed into a dresser corner and all my bottom teeth went through my lip.
(2) Good swimmer.
(3) [blank]

That they have far less detailed and intriguing "stories," that they put down only the most cursory of information about themselves, and that all four cannot come up with a single interesting "fact" that they know, is telling. Does this mean that the roots of poetry go deep into the stories we're told, with taking on the idiosyncrasies of personality (versus the bland, general facts, such as "good swimmer" or "cheerleading") and a rich curiosity about the small stuff of the world? Or do these students often invest less of themselves in schoolwork, especially when there's no grade involved? Small interest yields small investment: why think of a story or a personal fact when something generic will do just as well? And yet another possibility could be that writing such things down doesn't intrigue them. Jenny, who carefully spelled out how ants can enslave other ants, might naturally veer toward enjoying writing.

Small weaknesses aside, all this sharing brought me closer to them from the very start. Maybe it just became a way of saying: poetry is a place for the idiosyncratic and the personal, along with the mysterious particularities of life. We weren't writing a poem that day, although I'd intended to (I threw out that plan as soon as I saw the rich material that was emerging). Instead, we were opening up a territory and forming a community. We were saying: it is okay to be you, with just your background and just your odd interests and knowledge. The table of literature, poetry, and art is one you can bring your full self to. And it's okay to laugh.

Lesson 18: Mockingbird Moments

After our introductory session with facts and stories, I spent my first few days with the classes as "just another student," reading *To Kill a Mockingbird* at the pace they did, taking the quizzes, and participating in discussions. Reading the novel became an experience itself in reading metaphor, with layers of connection we learned to walk in and out of. Indeed, it almost seemed to me that Jill was teaching us all to read for the first time, asking us to slow down our pace and take in the subtleties of moments. One morning she asked us to look at a passage where Scout is falling asleep after the jail incident and in her half-waking state sees the image of her father calmly folding his newspaper blur into the scene of him pushing up his glasses before he shoots the rabies-mad dog earlier in the story. I realized I'd skipped right over that parallel. The students had too, apparently, as it took a lot of coaxing for anyone to see what Harper Lee meant. I wondered what else we were missing.

Following Jill's lead, on Friday, September 27, as an introduction to my first writing lesson with the classes, I began by asking: "Why read a novel like this?" To my surprise, for so bright a class, they had very little to say. Maybe they were a little shocked by my question. Jenny said: "Because **she** wants us to. . . . " There was more resentment in her voice than I'd ever have imagined. Other answers followed suit: "Because it's good for us." "Because it's on the list of books to read." "Because we're AP and other kids can't." Only Amber was able to come up with something more meaningful: "Because it might give us lessons we can look back to later in our lives." That's something of what I had in mind, thinking about the scene in *The Great Gatsby* in which Daisy hits Myrtle with

Gatsby's car and just keeps on going—and she and her husband Tom cover up her guilt, eventually pinning it on Gatsby, ultimately causing his death. Fitzgerald talks about the speed with which they lived, not giving them time to go back and reconsider what they've done. "They were careless people, Tom and Daisy—they smashed up things and creatures and then retreated back into their money . . . " is the way his narrator Nick Carroway puts it (180–181). As another example, Jill brought up the scene in *King Lear* in which the aging monarch is asking his daughters to praise him—and proceeds to disinherit his favorite daughter Cordelia because she won't play the game of buttering him up the way her superficial sisters do. With such moments in hand, we were suggesting, literature gives us the means to weigh our lives. We can ask: *When was I like that? Am I looking for flattery here more than genuine feeling? Have I, in some way, "run over people" on my way to success?* And it strikes me now: we were asking them to engage literature as a metaphoric process in itself, a place we can go for images, characters, gestures, and scenes to serve as measuring sticks for our own behavior, our own dreams.

First, though, we have to experience the story on some level beyond mere plot. As a start, it may help to visualize the novel as a series of moments we can "walk around in." At least that was the premise Jill and I presented to the kids, using poetry as a means to "stop time." We asked them to pick a character and write a poem in his or her voice at a single moment in the novel, not explaining who is talking, just letting the character and the moment come through in the description and voice. We used Ann Stanford's poem "The Blackberry Thicket" as an example of a poem strongly evoking the fullness of a single experience through detail and metaphor. (See the following for the full text.)

Each line in her poem adds a strand to the picture as she places us in the scene from the opening on:

> I stand here in the ditch, my feet on a rock in the water
> Head-deep in a coppice of thorns

She gives us enough details to establish location and presence, then proceeds to spin out memories, references, and sensory evocations:

> Remembering stains—
> The blue of mulberry on the tongue
> Brown fingers after walnut husking—

I hoped the kids would take from her example the notion of filling their poems with the senses—a tough thing to do for high school sophomores, for it's the "big ideas" that often matter most to them. Stanford gives us some of these as well:

> Here I am printed with the earth
> Always and always the earth ground into the fingers

but she couples such grand thoughts with the simplicity of the place as well:

> Surely not alone
> I stand in this quiet in the shadow
> Under a roof of bees.

Most of all, maybe it was the experience of *hearing* a poem that I wanted them to achieve at this moment. So little of what they've heard or read out in the world, or in school itself, will have had this sort of evocative, up-in-the-air feeling. There is no "great message" in Stanford's poem, just the honoring of standing on a rock in a stream, picking berries overhead. I wanted them to recognize the subtle use of sensory language (the stain of mulberry, the juice of the blackberries), and I wanted them to feel that wonderful sense of the "box clicking shut" at the end of the poem, the finish that is also open-ended, the metaphorical surprise of "a roof of bees." It is, most of all, *experience* that this poem honors, the way John Dewey says all art begins with paying attention to the nature of experience itself, "recovering the continuity of aesthetic experience with normal processes of living."

A Poem for Writing about Moments

I include the whole text of Ann Stanford's wonderful "moment poem" here because it's so useful in many contexts for modeling for us how to be in a moment and how to let quiet things resonate. It works for helping students wander out into the woods, or into a painting, or back into their own memories, or, as we will see, into the text of a novel.

The Blackberry Thicket

> I stand here in the ditch, my feet on a rock in the water,
> Head-deep in a coppice of thorns,
> Picking wild blackberries,
> Watching the juice-dark rivulet run
> Over my fingers, marking the lines and the whorls,
> Remembering stains—
> The blue of mulberry on my tongue,
> Brown fingers after walnut husking,

And the green smudge of grass—
The earnest part
Of heat and orchards and sweet springing places.
Here I am printed with the earth
Always and always the earth ground into the fingers,
And the arm scratched in thickets of spiders.
Over the marshy water the cicada rustles,
A runner snaps sharp into place.
The dry leaves are a presence,
A companion that follows up under the trees of the orchard
Repeating my footsteps. I stop to listen.
Surely not alone
I stand in this quiet in the shadow
Under a roof of bees.

—Ann Stafford

By writing one moment from the novel, as much in the voice of the character as they could, I hoped they'd deepen their experience of all such moments. Here's part of what Corky jotted down:

Jem's Amusement

As I stand, shaking away my branches, I realize that I'm at the Radley's house. I approach, feeling droplets push through my pores as I start to get closer. It seems like hours. When I finally get to the door, I raise my hand, feeling like an anchor.

It's not perfect. It plods. And "It seems like hours" is a distancing cliché. But "feeling droplets push through my pores" . . . now *that's* nice. It captures the slow motion without telling us it's slow, as does the hand feeling like an anchor. Over and over, with their early poems, I see it happening: their metaphors when they work are *physical*, and physicality grounds the writing, letting it slink past generality and turning us closer toward full experience. Is this part of what the process of reading literature slowly accomplishes—giving us time to "catch up with ourselves," not always racing for "the big lessons" but dwelling in the details long enough to let them connect with physical presence and *then* with idea? Kelley writes, thinking of Scout listening in on her father's conversation with men who come to warn him of trouble down at the courthouse:

I press my
face against the screen
as if I was being
suctioned into their
conversation

Here is the true surprise of metaphor, for Kelley's words suggest a powerful image of Scout feeling she's in two places at once—hidden away in her childhood on one side of the screen and out in Atticus's adult and dangerous world on the other.

Josh's metaphors are more evasive and clever, getting closer to the heart of Jem's hatred at having to read to Mrs. Dubose as punishment for destroying her flowers:

> Knocking on the chamber door
> An answer
> Skulking, hit by a breeze of dragon's breath
> Dark, gloomy, a hint of courage or death
> Holding my sentence in my hand
> I enter
> wretched visions
> I start to slay

A riddle so hidden, in fact, that at first I don't get it. Then I see: he is able to metaphorize every tiny bit, the chamber door calling up medieval scenes, as does his reference to dragon's breath for Mrs. Dubose's fierce words. "My sentence in my hand" refers to the books Jem is required to read to her for a month as atonement. Even Jem's reading, then, is a kind of "slaying."

What else but metaphor can achieve this inside view? How can we hear the resonance of Jem's task until we see it through the eyes of the reader? It appears that approaching a more engaged world view necessitates finding our own metaphors for *any* experience, even ones we obtain vicariously through reading a novel.

Is there only one way to achieve this? Clearly not. Look at how Jenny avoids the flourish of descriptive metaphor completely, sticking to a steady pace of inner monologue as she describes Atticus approaching the mad dog:

> Are you really
> Ready for this?
> You're going to have
> To do it sometime
> Take your time
> Glasses up
> Who cares?
> Hands firm
> Focus
> Steady now
> Always was
> Just a little
> To the right

Maybe sometimes all a poem has to do is *hold thought still enough* for us to climb inside. We certainly feel her there, standing, as it were, in Atticus's shoes. Thus Jenny's metaphor could be said to contain the whole experience of being *that steady,* as she herself may have to be someday, pitching a softball game or standing before her own courtroom.

Ideally, one would put the two skills together, as Brian does in his poem about the death of Mr. Ewell, written a couple weeks later after we'd done additional work in metaphor and physical detail.

Mr. Ewell

The cool drink is like a morning dewdrop
to my tongue. But I don't taste it.
The smell of fall rushes through my nostrils,
but I don't smell it.
My mind is as focused as I can,
here with this bottle in my hand.
I hear some children talking—it's HIS boy.
My nose boils and I start following them in
this blue-black darkness.
They stop, I stop, I feel the cold shine of
the metal on my thigh. I pull it out, and grin
wickedly.
This is best served cold!
I race at them, but the boy hears me. That ain't
right, he has a ham?
He hits me but I hit him harder. He falls . . .
I slice at the ham.
I twist his arm and hear a crack, like a branch
snapping in a high wind.
Someone else is here, I hear them, I turn
but trip, I put my hand out, but this cold, hard
metal was waiting . . . I fall, never thinking, but
I feel something hit my stomach.
The knife had been waiting . . . for me.

Notice how much more *full* the portrait is now. Yes, it's more narrative, but it's also more fully absorbed into a single character's mind—and a villain's mind at that. Notice the *sensory* shifts and surprises: the beer compared to a dewdrop, his nose "boiling," and "the cold shine of the metal," mixing sight and touch so quietly. Even the "branch snapping in a high wind" conveys a sense of the motion and danger involved in the scene. And Brian has picked up some of Jenny's internal pacing as well, as in: "That ain't right, he has a ham?" I can hear Ewell saying this to himself. I can sense his internal revenge in "It's HIS boy."

Jill says she teaches this novel to encourage in students a healthy respect for the ability to "step in someone else's shoes," Atticus's code of honor—just as Jenny and Brian (and so many others) have done. In her essay, "Metaphor and Memory," Cynthia Ozick calls metaphor a moral device, helping us to permit the stranger—or the different point of view—into our thinking. As "the shocking extension of the unknown into our most intimate, most feeling, most private selves," Ozick says, "metaphor is the enemy of abstraction" (282). So Brian has let the stranger in, the alternative view, as well as breaking through the abstraction of "villain" into some living, breathing understanding. If disengagement can in some sense mean being wrapped up in our abstractions, in our own little worlds, reading this novel with Jill became for us a first step in "doing otherwise," in approaching the world through multilayered, metaphorically rich lenses.

Applying the Lesson on Your Own

Surely "entering a moment in a novel" in poem form can be adapted to almost any level. I've tried it with advanced twelfth graders who had recently read Moby Dick *(from which we created a staged readers-theater production), as well as with fifth graders, who chose moments from their SSR books.*

First, take a close look at a couple of "moment in time" poems, such as Gary Snyder's "Mid-August at Sourdough Mountain Lookout" (p. 30) or James Wright's "Milkweed" (p. 150), then ask students to choose their own, recreating their moments with sensory detail and well-crafted metaphors. It's a great way to study any *novel from multiple points of view.*

Lesson 19: Metaphor and the Mind

On the way to persona poems like Brian's there were, of course, a number of other smaller steps, specifically in developing attention to metaphor. We looked at clips from the film version of *To Kill a Mockingbird* and tried to view them metaphorically. We asked students to take sections of poems and create shot-by-shot film scripts for how they visualized the poem. The biggest breakthrough, though, was a spur-of-the-moment idea I stumbled upon while seeking to make the connection between the kind of metaphors we do in poetry and the ones that appear in prose.

After Jill had called our attention to the mad-dog/angry-crowd image, I realized the book was more layered with metaphor than I'd ever imagined. In the middle of one lesson, on a hunch, I said: "Hunt through the book and find a metaphor somewhere and read it to us." When this went slowly, I made it even more specific: "Put your finger down *anywhere* in the book—on any paragraph—and see if you find a metaphor there." Only at that point did the lesson sink home. Left and right around the room hands were up, stumbling over each other to ask, "Is this one?" or announce, "I think I've got one here." Here's a sampling:

> Sarah M.: "Dill was a villain's villain." (44)
>
> Brittany: "It was over. We bounded down the sidewalk on a spree of sheer relief." (110)
>
> Sara G.: "Summer was the swiftness with which Dill would reach up and kiss me when Jem was not looking." (116)
>
> David F., locating a clue to Atticus's calmness under pressure: "In a group of neighbors, Atticus was standing with his hands in his overcoat pockets. He might have been watching a football game." (70)
>
> Even Garrison, who often acted disconnected from the poetry, seemed pleased with his discovery of "Atticus's voice was flinty." (30)
>
> And Emma, so often attuned to the deeper moral questions, found one that touched on the theme of racial bias so central to the book, noting how black people's homes were referred to by one character as "nests," implying a certain animal nature to their lives. (175)

And I noticed the phrase where Scout stays behind after lunch "to advise Atticus about Calpurnia's inequities." Even the verb *advise* becomes metaphorical here, suggesting a role she's taken on of "lawyering" her lawyer father.

Everywhere we looked metaphor was at work, shaping the tone of a verb and suggesting connections, textures, and character traits with quiet aplomb. When I look back on the semester, I think this was perhaps *the* single most important event for showing the value of what we were doing. No longer was metaphor just a pretty poetic device, but quite at the heart of good sentence construction.

To continue our exploration of metaphor, we read Patricia Fargnoli's poem, "How This Poet Thinks," which begins,

I don't think
like lawyers, quick in the mind,
rapid as a rat-a-tat-tat,
or academics, who pile up logic
like wood to get them through the winter.

I think the way someone listens
in a still place for the sound of quiet—

and which includes lines like:

When I think, sometimes it is
like objects rushing through a tunnel,
and sometimes
it is like water in a well with dirt sides,
where the wetness is completely absorbed

and the ground rings with dampness,
becomes a changed thing.

Then we tried lines of our own based on the phrase, "My mind is like. . . ."
I asked them to stretch their ideas, the way she does, not just naming
what their minds were like, but saying *how* in a second phrase or two.
Perhaps this let them apply in a direct way all the abstractions we'd been
talking about earlier.

Here are some results:

My mind is like a river,
running through the woods,
turning until it reaches
a grudge.

                    —Ci'Arra

My mind is like a birdie in a badminton match
always changing direction

                    —Heather

My mind is like an ocean—large, loud, watery.
My mind is like a leather glove—rough, tough, worn.

                    —David F.

My mind is like a restaurant,
Always serving me something new
Once one thing is finished, another begins
Never closed, open 24 hours

                    —Lauren

My mind is like a cat with yarn or a baby with clattering keys
It opens like a crowbar, rusted & aged, would a once locked door

                    —Josh

What Wheelwright would call "tensive language" is beginning to work here. Think of it as the ability to put a twist on each phrase—to surprise. Ci'Arra's grudge, for instance; that single word changing the flow of her river-mind, the way we hold onto something that bugs us and won't let it go. Heather's badminton birdie is seemingly accurate for her changes in moods. David's ocean and leather glove images are added onto with the quick words that follow. Josh's crowbar line, which even with (or because of!) its disruptive punctuation models, what it is trying to show is the opening of new thought from a once-locked space.

There were of course plenty of less insightful lines. One student wrote, "My mind is like a door, an open door," and another, "My mind is like the sky—my thoughts go on forever." Yet even on the most minimal shift, some energy can be felt. Ashley S. wrote, "My mind is like a flower, alive." I told her I liked how much importance falls on that last word. From that single gesture, as we will see in future examples, it seems her poetry started to grow.

To reengage the world, we might begin with trying to define the nebulous recesses of our own minds, using metaphor to suggest possible ways of physicalizing the unseen processes we go through when we think. In doing so, our minds became ACTIVE places, filled with shifts and gestures, migrations and erasures. If our individual minds are as radically different as these poems suggest, perhaps it is okay to be ourselves, while at the same time appreciating the different minds around us. In one of the "exit interviews" I did with students at the end of the semester, two interviewees looked back on this assignment as a place where they discovered how to say something about yourself in a poem but not be too revealing, appreciating how others had done the same. When we read back Nate's lines,

> My mind is like a thick cement block
> not easily changed or manipulated
> My mind is like my mother
> always getting ignored when it gives me orders . . .

We could laugh with him at his self-depreciating good humor and yet realize he's being quite honest.

Jordan does something of the same when he writes:

> My mind is slow like the snail that is
> bogged down by its worldly possessions.
>
> My mind is a child—it only sees the obvious
> and leaves out the details
> for fear of pain.

My mind is sharp and swift but not always
accurate as is the ax blade that pierces the
cherry tree.

In these well-hewn lines, Jordan has shown that he knows himself well, in his strengths and his weaknesses. Such two-way recognition could be another important step toward more fully reengaging the power of words.

Applying the Lesson on Your Own

While this lesson is mostly self-explanatory, I'd suggest first taking any recent, well-written text the class had read and trying the same "scavenger hunt for metaphors" in preparation. I'd also suggest using the full text of Patricia Fargnoli's poem, available in her book Necessary Light, *along with finding a copy of Ted Hughes's "The Thought-Fox" as a supplementary example.*

Another step might be to use a word bowl, having students draw from it, with the requirement that they weave in at least five of the words they find into making the comparisons for "what their minds are like."

Lesson 20: Earth Water Fire and Air

After one assignment focusing on a novel and another making wild comparisons for what their minds might be like, we felt it was time to tap into the students' own experiences as sources for their poems. For this next lesson, I asked them to make lists of moments they could recall that involved earth, water, fire, and air. Water might come in the form of ice or snow, of course; or at the edge of the ocean or in the form of a childhood bath. Air might involve shadows and light and open windows as well as a flight in a hot-air balloon. Fire might be a friend or a foe. Earth, that silent presence in everything we do, could be a mountain climbed or the influence of gravity we're made aware of after a hard fall. Setting their memory lists aside, I next asked them to read around in our class anthology of poems, looking particularly at a series of poems that emphasized the four elements of earth, water, fire, and air. What followed was one of the most wonderful events in any classroom: ten minutes of absorbed and silent reading, from which we took suggestions for which poem they most wanted to talk about. One class chose a playful poem called "Whales" by Harley Elliott, the other leaned toward Christopher Merrill's more ominous poem, "Childhood." We marked in the first how the "quality of sleep in bathtubs" gives way to visions of "the sun fading out forever/above the deepening layers of light" until eventually the speaker imagines us "down among the whales / as they pass their squeaking / banshee songs swell[ing] / beneath the green black sea" (55). I was hopeful that such lines would show them the soft touches metaphor could take, lifting us out of ordinary knowing and into an awareness of being connected to things and creatures far beyond our immediate worries.

The choice of the second class, Christopher Merrill's poem, achieves something of the same effect, though in a more troubling way:

Childhood

Newspapers scarred the stream;
Words swirled in the eddies;
Grey figures—a dead thief,
The President and his wife,
Two race horses—floated past
And sank . . .
Or snagged the rocks
Rippling the slow water
Until the sun, like a man
With a knife, cut them apart
So they could sail away.

     . . .

On the last night, outside my tent, someone
Startled the woods: a flashlight fluttered; twigs,
Like small animals, crackled underfoot;
Mosquitoes buzzed the netting. I held my breath
To hear the hushed voices, a muffled cough,
A siren down the road . . .
A match was struck,
I crawled outside: my mother and my father,
Dressed in white, stood near the sumac, waving
Their hands of fire. They touched the trees, they licked
Their palms, and rose above the burning woods.

What a discussion we had about this poem! People saw the invasion of "the news" in the opening line, foreshadowing as it does the death of President Kennedy. Some saw the second half of the poem as a dream; others thought it symbolic of losing his parents to the wider world (of politics, of work, of his own growing up).

Finally, we had just enough time to glance at Susan Mitchell's "Blackbirds," with its mystical, almost fairy-tale evocation of "air":

Because it is windy, a woman
finds her clothesline bare, and without rancor
unpins the light, folding it into her basket . . .

Looking back, I think I subconsciously wanted to move them to a new level of writing, one in which the surprise and creative weirdness of their "mind" poems blended with their actual experiences to evoke a more magical worldview; one in which myth and fantasy was not so alien to daily routine. In some ways, all that transpired on this day built the groundwork for the inventive work they would do over the next few weeks.

Heidegger on Art and the Elemental

Martin Heidegger—philosopher and author of Being and Time*—contends that art's main role is to return us to some sense of our original relationship to be-ing and all that "earth" entails. "Earth," in his framework, is everything we as humans do not create or control, including rock, blood, rivers, lava, ocean, mountains, sky, ozone, the animal world, and our own hearts; even, perhaps, our language—or at least the human propensity toward language, whatever the style of speech. All this is our "given," as well as our not-fully-knowable, base. Opposed to this unknowable basis of all that is, Heidegger places "World," within which he groups all that WE create—shoes and skyscrapers, school sys-tems and laws, highways and money and swimming pools, etc. We adapt the forces of the planet to our own use, and "use" is a keyword here. We use the earth, but we don't/can't fully know it. Art, Heidegger says, is our bridge that serves, according to two commentators on his theory, "as a kind of interface site, a meeting place of human purposes and decisions and their un-masterable, non-human horizon" (Collins and Selina, 133).*

Here are a few of their earth-water-fire-and-air poems. Bethany's, for instance, is something of an ode to fishing:

The Lure

Planted like a tree on the edge of the bank
My box of traps is my accomplice
Ripples, clouds that come and linger
Shifty and uncertain, it moves along . . .
and comes back,
it is also my secret friend.

The light plays with my senses
My mind drifts and is consumed
The immaculate display of whim . . .
I am a willing captive.

Now all the preparation in metaphor and moment, and physical detail and internal voice comes to fruition for Bethany for the first time. The lines themselves are playful, they linger, and they are secretive, revealing just enough to know she is fishing. It is, as she implies, herself she has caught here, *planted* in a place and activity she knows from the inside.

So too with Heather, who'd told me earlier she'd rather live almost anywhere else. Her parents had moved out to the country specifically because she had loved horses at age five. Now she's into the Internet and makeup, fashion shows and malls. Yet she's able to step back into a time of what could only be called "mud":

Building Our House

From the ground up we built it
The rocky earth was shifted, heaped, and moved
Until we found its position satisfactory
At first it was just a hole in the ground
But later it would become much more

The summer rains turned it into the mud puddle of a giant
Winter would bring icy winds
And freeze the earth solid

I can still hear the low hum then roar
Of the space heater
I can still smell the burning leaves

For a kid not so much in love with horses or the country anymore, she sure is capable of recalling that time, the time her parents built a home—for her. Yet she doesn't talk *about* it; she gives us the rocky earth being "shifted, heaped, and moved." She also evokes a bit of magic, as a child then might have seen it, the giant's mud puddle, and sensed it—the mud frozen solid, the sound of the space heater, and the smell of the burning leaves.

Even the students' metaphors were getting sharper as a result of engaging sensory elements. Sarah S. wrote just three lines:

Small waves lick my toes
like fire to a log
consuming me as tides rise . . .

Yet those three lines are more valuable than a dozen, containing as they do the surprising twist of calling the ocean a fire. It's nearly a surreal move, comparing herself to a log burning. If the ocean is often compared to a releasing force that overwhelms our "solid" consciousness, Sarah has given us a small memento of that change.

Memory kicks in, too, as Sarah M. recalls a childhood friend who had the wind knocked out of her during a fall in gym class:

Climbing a tree or a rope

I hold fast to the earth as
I move up through the air. Knowing
if I were to let go, the air
would pass right through me, & I'd
be back to where the air
began.

How much more could she say about that experience? She's caught distance, fear, even a bit of elation (as the fall might feel), and certainly a ton of mystery in that last line: "& I'd be back to where the air / began."

Perhaps because of Christopher Merrill's poem, perhaps because of its ancient aura, fire drew the most writers to it that day in impressively different ways. Here Brittany finds it as a metaphor for some disappointment in her own life:

The Fire

Sitting there glowing in the night,
How I got here I don't know
People standing all around me rubbing their hands
They're relying on me to keep them warm
I start to flicker and shrink
A man grabs a stick and starts to poke at me
Trying to stay strong for their sake,
I just don't have the power to
So slowly I start to die
As I feel I've disappointed them

It was only reading that poem aloud to the class the next meeting—and looking back at Brittany—that I felt how much the poem didn't just take on the voice of fire (as I'd thought on first reading); but rather, the fire took on the voice of *her.* At that moment I understood something new, something very metaphorical and sociologically true: how we can poke and prod at our children, asking them to keep us awake and warm, when maybe they just don't want to.

Here's one more poem of fire, one based in reality, though it might feel like a dream . . .

Memory of South Carolina

Going down the long winding
country road once more
I can almost see the blaze

before we can reach it.
I feel the heat
consuming me, wrapping itself
around me like a soft blanket
made of fine sheep's wool.
Reaching the climax of the hill, I
see small tips of gold and sun-dipped
red reminding me of the last rays of
sunshine before earth elopes with total
darkness.
Now I can see plain as the
dashboard of the car, the fire.
A blaze, that comforting oblivion
Of yellows and reds and oranges
stretching for acres
swallowing the rich green earth.

—Amber

I wanted to hug her and yell out, "Amber's first really strong poem!" We're almost able to see the fire before getting there, in some kind of premonition, as well as receiving the strange, ironic comfort of the heat wrapping itself around her. Then there is the line that most makes the poem for me: her twist on the old familiar phrase "plain as the nose on my face . . ." but no, she turns it and appropriately makes it "plain as the dashboard of the car," lit up as it is with its own internal fire.

Applying the Lesson on Your Own

I've found this lesson to be adaptable to a wide range of students, from fifth grade on up to college, from rural to suburban to inner city areas. I often start with a discussion of the ways such elements have long been a part of human life over the centuries, and we make a list of ways people have used them, followed by a second list of how those of us in the "industrialized world" use them somewhat differently now. The next trick is to collect a range of poems that strongly make use of one of these elements. Finally, when it comes to writing, I've usually offered them three options: (1) to choose a memory of their own and write it out in a poem form; (2) to write a dream of that element; or (3) to become the element, *writing from its voice. Those students who have been camping, or canoeing, or have worked on a farm or in a garden have one set of memories from which to draw. Those with more city-bound experiences have another set, equally connected to the elements, just in different ways.*

Lesson 21: Supposing

The time came to be more radically playful. On Thursday morning, two days after our session with the "elements," I got up, against my habit, at 4 a.m., feeling something was wrong with the plan we'd concocted for the day. I had a gut feeling we needed to move on now from memory and personal experience, but where next? Then I thought of **play**, the sort of wordplay we'd done when we came up with metaphors for what "my mind is like . . . " but had not had a chance to return to or build on; the play with sound I'd been wanting to squeeze in all along. The assignment that arose was perhaps the result of not enough sleep and disturbing the shadows in our basement at such an early hour, yet somehow—perhaps because of one keyword: "suppose"—it proved to be the most fun we'd had so far.

In my sleeplessness I came in and announced, "THE UNIVERSE IS PLAYFUL," chalking it in capital letters across the board. Playful, I told them, as Atticus keeps his wits about him before the crowd of vengeful and racist men gathered at the prison to lynch Tom Robinson, and playful as Mr. Tate who at the end of the novel has to ignore the law a little to avoid a pointless trial for Boo Radley.

Because I was in the mood for a deeper connection with the students, I told two stories. One was about the time my first wife Carla and I rode our bikes across the country, in preparation for when I sold my old green Raleigh 10-speed to buy a 15-speed Schwinn that could handle the mountains more easily. I sold it to a geology major at Wittenberg University in Springfield, Ohio, a stranger whom I never expected to see again. Then, a couple of months or so later, riding across the plains of Wyoming, just a little ways past the Grand Tetons, we heard one of the few cars to pass us for miles turn around and circle back, only to pull up right beside us. Having been warned to be careful of people who had been harassing bikers in this mainly deserted territory, I cringed, wondering how to defend ourselves against an assault. The driver called out, and it was only then that I looked over to see my green Raleigh mounted on a rack on top of his car. We stopped and talked. Apparently he was on his way to a geology seminar up in the Tetons, at a place we'd passed ten miles back. Had we been fifteen minutes later getting up that day, he'd have already turned in the driveway by the time we got there. As it was, we got a little taste of how playful the universe can be.

The second story concerned something far more serious—the death of my mother that past August. Without going into details about her illness, which was mercifully brief, and her life of eighty-one years, which was blessedly long and beautiful, I told them what happened when I drove up to see her at the hospital in Michigan a week before she died. On the way, as we are wont to do, I put in a tape to pass the time, reaching behind me into the tape box and for some odd reason deciding I'd just "take whatever I got," but secretly hoping it was by Greg Brown. It was by him, but not the tape I thought I had. It was, instead, "The Poet's Game," which I'd forgotten recording off a CD a few years ago. I listened to nearly the end of the first side, coming to the last phrases of the last song as I turned off the headlights in the parking lot.

I met my brother in the corridor about 9:30 p.m., as he was heading home. He told me her stroke was worse than we'd thought. We hugged (a rare occurrence for us), and I stayed with Mom until 11:30 or so, deciding then to drive out to my parents' house and get some sleep myself. I knew I was tired from the long drive and, worried as I was, I didn't know what else I could do right then. She was breathing evenly, but not responding to any contact. Out on Grand River Avenue, I called my wife Leslie from the cell phone, and then decided to listen to the rest of the Greg Brown tape—again, as we are wont to do, even at times like these, thinking to fast-forward through to the other side. But for some reason, I reached out to stop the forwarding button, in case I'd missed something—*and my mom's voice came on.* It was an interview my daughter Isa had done with her a few years before for a college project. Mom was talking about one of her pet peeves—about why people can't get along with each other better (I'd always ribbed her about that naïveté). But here's the point: I didn't even know I had that tape, much less recorded "The Poet's Game" over it. And had I just let it fast-forward, I never would have known. Nor would I have suddenly realized that this might be my daughter's grandmother's last weekend alive, and I immediately called Isa, asking her to come up the very next day. She did and was able to play her violin for her grandmother one last time and make her a last dinner.

Call either of these incidents—and dozens others like them—coincidences. I prefer to think of them as the universe playing—as Frost said—for mortal stakes. Perhaps I wanted to bring a little bit more mystery into the room. I said that poetry was one way we get to play with mystery—and one way we can begin that is to play with language, opening it up after all the daily stuff we do with words to close them in and make them stale.

This was a long introduction to a rather unserious exercise. Here's the game sheet for what we did next, a game you might call Scrambling the Sounds:

1. Pass out 35 blank cards to each "player."

2. Have each person put "concrete nouns" on the first ten, each word with a strong B, D, G, K, P, or T sound (called the mutes and said by many people, including Mary Oliver, to be the strongest sounds in the language, especially for poetry).

3. Shuffle these cards and deal out four to yourself, leaving the blank cards aside.

4. For each of these four words, come up with three words that "alliterate" with it, either for the first letter or for other strong letters (for "strum," for instance, one might add three cards with "middle," "song," and "strike"). The only hint here would be to keep the words as physically or concretely based as possible. At this point, you will have twenty-two cards.

5. Now, add five active, interesting verbs from your blank cards. You will then have twenty-seven word cards.

6. Shuffle all the cards-with-words-on-them again and draw out four more, adding two "half-rhymes" for each (half-rhymes being words that almost rhyme, but not quite—such as "leaf" having *some* of the sound of "life," but not all; they can add a subtle new texture to poems, without the reader being so blatantly made aware of it, as with full rhyme).

This should give you a deck of thirty-five words, each with at least a certain amount of sound potential in relationship to the other words.

Any number of poems could be written from these words. My original idea was to have them write a poem of sixteen lines, using two words from their pack in each, but that got shifted over the course of the day to "Write a poem of whatever length, using at least two of your words in each line, with every line or so starting with the word, "Suppose. . . ." I used as a model a somewhat long poem by Pattiann Rogers, "Suppose Your Father Was a Redbird." I've loved it for quite some time as an example of a poet thinking freely while still making a compelling point. Besides that, it's full of good sound and a sort of metaphor that I thought would stretch the students at this point. I don't know a better example of a poem that steps us out of our purely human, narrow seeing and into participating in experience with all our senses. Her imagery, so richly physical and surprising, and deeply majestic, is based not only in the eye but in the body, the body of a nested fledgling.

Suppose Your Father Was a Redbird

Suppose his body was the meticulous layering
Of graduated down which you studied early,
Rows of feathers increasing in size to the hard-splayed
Wine-gloss tips of his outer edges.

Suppose, before you could speak, you watched
The slow spread of his wing over and over,
The appearance of that invisible appendage,
The unfolding transformation of his body to the airborne.
And you followed his departure again and again,
Learning to distinguish the red microbe of his being
Far into the line of the horizon.

Then today you might be the only one able to see
The breast of a single red bloom
Five miles away across an open field.
The modification of your eye might have enabled you
To spot a red moth hanging on an oak branch
In the exact center of the Aurorean Forest.
And you could define for us, "hearing red in the air,"
As you predict the day pollen from the poppy
Will blow in from the valley.

Naturally you would picture your faith arranged
In filamented principles moving from pink
To crimson at the final quill. And the red tremble
Of your dream you might explain as the shimmer
Of his back lost over the sea at dawn.
Your sudden visions you might interpret as the uncreasing
Of heaven, the bones of the sky spread,
The conceptualized wing of the mind untangling.

Imagine the intensity of your revelation
The night the entire body of a star turns red
And you watch it as it rushes in flames
Across the black, down into the hills.

If your father was a redbird,
Then you would be obligated to try to understand
What it is you recognize in the sun
As you study it again this evening

Pulling itself and the sky in dark red
Over the edge of the earth.

Though we did not discuss the poem at all and merely heard it read aloud, I believe Rogers's complex language grounded us well. The poems that resulted surprised and pleased me immensely. They varied greatly but were all equally playful and inventive, not so much in the realm of sound, but banking off the sound of the words in order to combine them in intriguing ways. All swirling around that wonderful word "suppose . . . ."

A string of their lines might begin to give a sense of the flair they achieved:

> Suppose a paper clip began speaking,
> Laughing as it was brushing its teeth
>
> —Erin

> Suppose Dakota could stroke,
> Blackbirds could breathe,
> Suppose doors had names
>
> —David F.

> Suppose the bard had orange hair
> The horse's name was Shadow
> Your bedroom wall screams at you
> A monkey showed up at your door
> Suppose your head was smaller than your dog's
>
> —Kurtis

> Suppose you clasped a star
> Holding tight to you a light
> Making your heart soar
> Suppose you masked dying
>
> —Sarah S.

> Suppose you were dancing in flower fields
> Freezing, screaming, wishing you had some heat
> Wishing blankets would drown you
> And the fire would stay strong
> Pictures in the clouds of pumpkins and mushrooms
> Suppose you could stroke your smiling heart
>
> —Julie

Even as I type these again, I see at once more exuberance, more humor, more depth, and more joy in these than in anything we'd written so far. But before analyzing, I have to hear some more. The second class, for whatever reason, wrote more on the order of whole poems, as Sarah K. does here:

> Suppose the course of your life
> Was rearranged
> Instead of silence
> Screams could not be heard.
>
> Suppose being proud
> Was balanced with shame
> Would you be shameful
> Or forever dawned with pride?
>
> Suppose life was a paper clip
> An endless curve of fame
> Counted by every stroke
> To where you may arrive
>
> Suppose clouds were at your feet
> Cranes would never fall
> And raindrops never kissed the sky
> Would you wave a white flag
> Or surrender?

Sarah's lines here, as in a few others', are less silly but equally textured and turned. It's just that the play for her led her to more cosmic thoughts, each with a touch of unusual imagery, as in the line about the paper clip. (I should mention that I also threw in the rule of having people say words out loud every two minutes or so, for use within our poems as each writer saw fit—which is why *stroke* and *paper clip* repeat in the previous poems, and *laugh* or *flubber* in the following couple of lines.)

Here's Jordan, whose previous lines, "My mind is sharp and swift, but not always accurate / as is the axe that pierces the cherry tree," had impressed me:

> Suppose torture was common
> as common as the beat of a horse's gallop
> the gallop screaming darkening the night.
>
> Suppose dictation was like the tick of a watch
> with each tick it slashes your heart
> no longer free.
>
> Suppose you listen to the stroke of midnight
> reevaluating your place
> clasping to something you thought you had.
> Maybe we shouldn't suppose.

The philosopher Hans-Georg Gadamer claims that only in the play of art are we truly free. Maybe our little "suppose" game offered us a way to play with "what might be" and "reevaluating [our] place," as Jordan does here.

In the first class, by contrast, people veered toward single lines, stuffed with as many of the words from the cards as they could contain:

Suppose sleepy sunsets were sheets of silk
Suppose gallantly green gardens were swallowed
in darkness

—Amber

Suppose Christmas presents hung from pillows
Suppose the pinnacle of the beaming lamp ran away
Suppose the laugh of water could be heard all over

—Bethany

Suppose stampedes were clumsy
Suppose laughter had a temper

—Nate

Suppose a distant daylight dawned inside your brain

—Brian

Suppose you were a catdog and romped in the grass
You looking dark and flubbery

—Heather

Suppose all the stones were trees and all the trees
were stone as the water is cement and the bus is a camel
Turn fur into dogs or a dock into a giant bomb exploding
with a boom and a laugh, and every lock in the world was free

—Corky

Suppose everything you say rhymes with shoelace and whim
Suppose kings opened doors for others

—Brenna

Suppose you could look through the dark
and see the dog making its dreadful journey
Suppose you couldn't laugh or see beauty

—Rachel

Suppose your goal was to become a board

—Shelby

Suppose making was in the midst

—Ben V.

Suppose the ground sizzled the damp of the room

—Jenny

Suppose a sweater poked like a nail
Suppose flubber

—Lauren

I can't fully explain the day—and don't need to. Maybe my unconscious woke me from my sleep to tell me it was time to stop plodding through the "basic exercises" and come up with something new. If we are to keep our work in the classroom fresh, in the teaching of poetry or anything else, maybe there are times to simply "break the plan" this way. My friend poet Stuart Lishan, with whom I have concocted similar assignments during various weeklong summer workshops we've taught together, refers to such sudden shifts as "calling an audible," just as football quarterbacks sometimes recognize that the configuration of the defense requires a new move. Part of the excitement of the day—for me as well as the students—was just in that: trying something we hadn't done before.

All I know is that I drove home that day enthralled (tired but enthralled). There were, of course, many ways we had "played" with poetry already, according to the types of play outlined in the first part of this book. Several times we had taken on roles—of characters in the novel, or taking on the voice of "fire" as in Brittany's poem quoted earlier—and you could say we had played continually with metaphor. But this is the first work we'd done with conscious wordplay. And it seems unlikely that such combinations of ideas would have happened without the wide range of unrelated words we had in front of us. Would Jenny have thought of the "ground sizzling" without the 35-card deck and its range of shuffling possibilities? Would Brian have imagined a "distant daylight dawning in your brain"? Would Nate ever have thought of his wonderful insights, of stampedes being clumsy (aren't they?) or laughter having a temper (doesn't it?)? Would Shelby have made us laugh, imagining the goal of becoming a board? I doubt it. Not without the words—and Pattiann Rogers's gorgeously inventive worldview. It freed something inside of us—perhaps accounting for the sense of joy that leaps out of so many of their lines.

Applying the Lesson on Your Own

For classes that already have done quite a bit of writing—and need a spark—doing the word cards to explore half-rhyme, alliteration, and the mutes can be fairly liberating. It's so easy to get into "writing in the realm of the real" that it's invigorating to have a game give us permission to do otherwise. The "suppose" approach is not the only way to go, but it does provide an excellent skeleton upon which to build some intriguing lines. There's no predicting how your class will take the idea—toward sound play and humor, as one class did above, or toward more serious reflection, as the other did, or somewhere in-between. That's in the nature of "supposing," I suppose.

―――――

8 Out on the Town

Lesson 22: Writing about Local History

After many days investigating metaphor, play, and the physical world, it was time to pay more particular attention to the visual side of experience. We were lucky. Jill knew the Millers, Jim and Phyllis, who are the repository of much local history and who possess a terrific collection of historical photographs from the county (see Figure 8.1). With the Millers providing background and visual clues, students were able to invest their "projective" and metaphoric skills into scenes familiar enough to be appealing yet distant enough to cause them to speculate. Was it an engaged worldview? Perhaps a good place to start is with all that has been forgotten historically about the "worlds" where we actually live.

From the Millers we learned all sorts of intriguing facts about the Mt. Gilead area:

1. The name of the town, for instance, is so striking for a place with no noticeable hills, much less mountains! It turns out the town was named

Figure 8.1. Unknown photographer, "Phillips & Son"

after a place in Virginia that Sara Nichols, a resident in the 1840s, fondly remembered from her childhood.

2. For many years Main Street was shut down for winter sleigh races.

3. The name of one local butcher was Sister Vanatta—a rather whiskered individual for such a nickname.

4. The town once had the world's record for the shortest railroad line. The Short Line RR—from Mt. Gilead to Edison, only one-and-a-quarter miles away—made it possible for local residents to catch trains to Columbus, Cincinnati, and Cleveland after the town council refused to build a station for the railroad companies within the town itself. High school sports teams would travel to other districts by train way into the 1940s.

5. Up into the Millers's own childhoods, Friday and Saturday nights were booming gathering times on the city's streets, just as in many towns across America before the coming of malls and television. Bands would play in the center of the street. Teenagers would gather in their own groups while parents with small children used the streets for places to congregate and exchange news and ideas.

6. Two first-class hotels once anchored the downtown, attracting travelers as a midway stop between Cleveland and Columbus or Cincinnati, as Route 42 formed a main cross-state highway. *The* "place to work" for teens was as waitresses and porters in the Globe Hotel's restaurant and rooms (see Figure 8.2).

None of this is new information for those familiar with the progression of American life over the past fifty years. The story nonetheless woke up many of the students (and me, too). No wonder things seem so "boring and all the same" now, as many students had told me in interviews. They *are*—at least in comparison to all that had gone before. Walking the streets of Mt. Gilead, one is quite literally walking in a ghost town, or rather a town built on the top of ghosts, ones we never knew were there—until the Millers came with their collection of photographs and storehouse of knowledge.

Susan Sontag objects that photographs hide and disguise more than they reveal, desensitizing us to the complexities of what they promise to show. To that John Berger mostly agrees, but qualifies his response with these words of hope:

Figure 8.2. Unknown photographer, "The Globe Hotel"

> If we could begin to supply the contexts that the camera erases . . .
> we could come to be the camera's memory . . . [by using] words,
> comparisons, signs [to create] a context for a printed photograph.

Perhaps his prescription could be illustrated by what happened next.
For instead of lamely glancing through the photographs or typecasting
the scenes and people there in uninformed, assumptive ways, the stu-
dents had something of Berger's full context by which to enter what they
were seeing. They could use the metaphorizing skills they'd been work-
ing on, but couple them nicely with internalized background coming
from the Millers—and from their own curiosity and projection as to what
it was once like in this town they thought they knew so well. I would
say their poems, at their best, illustrate a kind of **engaged or informed
seeing**, informed by background and engaged with curiosity and a
newly learned ability to become a part of what they observe.

  After the Millers's background talk and slideshow, we distributed
a group of photographs the students had not seen yet, passing them out
randomly. Randomly, we said, because one doesn't always get to choose
where one lands in history. Rather we become—don't we—the person
that is possible within the circumstances we are handed. I asked them
to first look carefully at the scene before them, invoking all the skills
we'd been working on, and jot down notes along the following lines:

1. Jot down five intriguing details you notice in the photograph, everything from the way someone is standing or leaning (we can learn a lot from body language and gesture) to the objects and buildings that make up the scene.

2. Create at least three metaphors or similes for what something might look like or seem. A cloud, a street lamp, or a mound of hay might suggest all sorts of connections we sense but don't often articulate.

3. Come up with two questions about something you might not guess at first glance. (The Millers are here to respond to these.)

4. Come up with one or more "supposes" or inventions for what you CANNOT see in the photograph—something outside the frame or the timing of the picture.

I talked about how much photographs can exclude—which no doubt is way more than they include. They tell us some things but imply much more. If it's true that we contain all of history inside of us, photographs do too, being something like tiny islands in a vast sea of reference spreading around them, physically and culturally.

To my surprise and pleasure, the students jumped in. They were still high school sophomores after all, so they hung back at first, like swimmers before an immense, cold pool. But after I went up to Jim and asked him the location of the photograph I received, others followed suit nearly immediately, keeping both of the Millers busy with questions the rest of the hour. Even when the students began to write their poems, they would at times go up to check on a fact. It was like having a historical coach along to aid in the writing; one's own private informant to help spur the poem into being. If to respond or create art we need to "build the knowledge base," as art educator Sydney Walker claims, here we had our own knowledge base right beside us as we wrote.

Lawrence Raab and Maggie Anderson provided our best models for writing, with one poem taken directly from a photograph, and the other almost seeming to. Raab gives us the first, with his marvelously supple reading of:

An Old Photographer from Vermont

We are too far away to see the pattern
of the embroidery she holds against
the back of the chair in front of the house
with its open window and two screened doors.

Nor is her face clear, though she seems
to smile. Curves of a mountain blur off
to each side, and a pair of apple trees
press thin shade upon the walls.

It is late summer, blackberry season.

Beyond fields which we cannot see, a stream
burrows into the cool side of a hill. Further,
in wild country where she has never gone,
one dark pond reflects a circle of spruce,

and the birds are silent, for this is the time
just before a storm, when leaves grow heavy,
and your heart thickens for no reason.

Why, then, is she smiling,

as the first gust falls into the yard, as husband
or father calls from the house, telling her
to come in, far off telling her that, as

she strays into the crush of weeds, at the edge
of the field, beyond garden, barn, and all
of us. You would think she believes

the wind will carry her away.

Such lessons to be learned here! For Raab explores this photograph from
an array of viewpoints, letting us enjoy both the seeing of it and the
speculations about what is *not* shown. Where is the photograph itself
within the poem? Nicely evoked with a few touches of detail—the em-
broidery against the back of the chair, the "open window and two
screened doors." But beyond that window and within those doors, there
waits such ominous, compelling presences—a dark side in the scene
nearly spilling from within and the compelling other-world calling the
woman from without. We will see how Raab's model feeds its way down
into the students' own work, as he pauses to ask "what next" questions
("why, then, is she smiling") that guide his next speculation and dis-
covery.

Maggie Anderson, herself a confessed lover of photographs, sup-
plies us with a second "move." Instead of building outward, from the
center of the photograph to all the worlds beyond, Anderson begins with
the outer shell and steps within the frame of the photograph to specu-
late on what may be going on within. Here is her poem, "Kitchen Talk,"
which although not nominally about a picture, could easily be, so deftly
does it work within its frame:

Along the Outer Banks in North Carolina,
there is a grey house that rises from the tall
grasses and the sea oat like a tombstone.
Its hull is shedding. The rusted bell of the porch light
whistles out over the Sound.

An American flag on the roof twists
in white smoke; an osprey swoops in.
A dusty child's face is framed in the upstairs window
for an instant only.

Her brother's gone to Raleigh.

From my sandy spot by the highway I can almost hear it:
the kitchen talk inside.

Mama, how long'd you say
to cook that chicken?

Oh, I don't know, sister,
till it's done. Just till it's done.

The students seemed to love this poem, along with Raab's. Maybe
that in itself is telling. Together these poems offered a nice mix of in-
sider versus outsider writing, taking a scene and inferring stories within,
finding a precise way to compare—the house like a tombstone, the heart
thickening. The senses are brought into play as well: the flag twisting
in the smoke; the apple trees that "press thin shade upon the walls."
These are not dominantly dramatic poems. Together they say: small
things can matter; just as they do in a town like Mt. Gilead, just as the
Millers had been demonstrating.

Looking back on the students' poems from that day, it's often the
lists that guide their writing. Consider Jenny's approach to a photograph
of the city streets heaped with snow drifts (Figure 8.3), taking the shape
of two short poems:

Horses helping a woman across town
A face stares at you while you're
Walking down the frost-bitten streets
Wheels attempt turning on the packed powder

Clothing, Shoe, and Hat Stores
"Drugs, Books,
Wallpaper"

Two hands catch your eye: 3:41
You're forced to squint by the forceful
Shine of sugar

    ***

Campaigning
Snow
Shoe stores, Hat shops
Drinking fountain
Where are the power lines?
Where is the buggy driver?

Figure 8.3. Unknown photographer, "Snowy Street/Mt. Gilead"

> The snow is like a vacation, everything
> stops,
> yet you're free to
> do anything

No doubt it's clear that the second is the list that prepared her for the poem version above it. Yet I like the two takes together, the sketch revealing her internal brainstorming that helped the poem be more immediate and speculative.

Several of the students got posed photographs from patriotic events—a tough nut to crack, if you ask me, for there is no obvious story to explore, only the person (or the people) standing stiffly, staring, or smiling awkwardly into the camera. It's intriguing to consider how they chose to get out of such awkward boxes. Some of the poems become rather generic lists of facts. Ryan, for instance, gives us this simple list:

Morrow County Honor Roll

All the names
famous names
local names

> names of the ones you know
> names of people
> who served their country
> loyally
> you unlucky 37
> you lucky 1309
> who came back home

There is not much depth here. But what was he to do? Handed a photograph of a list of names, he invents a way in—or a way out. Where Ryan's poem takes on a certain subtle strength is in the two lines near the end that contrast the number killed (37) versus the ones who came home (1,309) from WWI. To lose thirty-seven men from one county stands out as significant—at least for those familiar with these "local names." Without creating a brilliant poem, Ryan has at the very least made a meaningful one out of a few basic observations and facts.

Matt is another student who had not stood out much in the poetry writing. He usually stayed in the land of the literal, as he does with these lines from his earth-water-fire-air memory piece, remembering his grandmother's farm:

> . . . Taking a dip in the swimming hole
> goofing around in the hay mow
> going in the house and getting some Disney popsicles
> seeing Dotty and Grandma Wegner playing board games
> catching fish with our bare hands
> walking along the stream
> having snowball fights
> sneaking Little Debbie treats from the cupboards . . .

He loves metonymy—one might even say passionately. I remember that he wanted very much to read his "Grandma Wegner" poem out loud to the class and was disappointed at the next session when I had typed up only a section of it, leaving off the pedantic opening and ending. But who am I to say? Maybe for him, poetry supplies a means of "keeping the world whole," versus a method to challenge our conventional views. I believe I lost Matt that day, earlier in the semester, as he realized that our two styles were so radically different. But look what he is able to do with this photograph of Casey Bending's garage (Figure 8.4):

Sportin' his ride

> A young man at the auto garage
> poses as the picture is taken.
> His arm spread out over his new Ford Model T.
> A spark in his eye
> and a crooked smile,

Figure 8.4. Unknown photographer, "Casey Bending Garage"

> not a happy smile but
> a proud smile.
> He runs his hand over the slick metal,
> a larger man in the background
> imitating the pose on the washed out stone
> wall.
> The young man smells the new car smell.
> He steps in and in a flash
> is gone from Casey Bending Garage.
> Suddenly a black blur appears on 42,
> and an arm waving in the air

As much as Matt would likely look back at the semester and call it a wash, and as much as I have to admit I did not get through to him, for whatever reason, we meet at this one point of intersection: we both like this poem. Maybe it was the influence of Raab and Anderson. Maybe it's the presence of the automobile. Maybe it's that it comes from his hometown, evoking the world of the men who made up this place eighty or so years ago. Whatever the reason, Matt became more *thorough* in his writing and observation here. He notices the driver's arm reaching out over ("spread out over") to the new car. He even makes a careful attempt to say what kind of smile the new owner has on his face.

I love how the students took to the photographs. And how their poems make those photographs come alive in my mind. Figure 8.5

Figure 8.5. Unknown photographer, "Sister Vanatta, Butcher"

shows the town butcher mentioned earlier, circa 1920, who apparently was nicknamed Sister Vanatta by his customers, possibly because of the apron he wore for his work. It's a posed piece, taken across a spotless counter, with a row of bloodless meat hanging along one wall and "Sister" standing before it like some sort of military sergeant presenting his troops. The photographer's flash has been caught in the storefront window, which is framed with fine oak woodwork and fan-like decoration. This is a clean shop, more like a living room or parlor than a slaughterhouse (one assumes that the actual butchering takes place in the back room anyway, or some other location). This is a photograph of *presentation*, a symbol of pride that Sister Vanatta could look to as a confirmation of his labor.

Sarah M. takes a look at these elements and then takes her poem a step further. She gets the facts across, establishing the scene in the first eight lines or so. She captures the sunlight, the cleanliness of the shop as opposed to the unwieldiness of the hanging meat, the ring of the register, and the reality of the daily sales. But notice how she makes it more personal in the last half . . .

Sister Vanatta

He keeps his shop so clean,
even though the freshly
cut meat hangs on the wall.
Only two lights to the room,
but the sun shines in so bright.
You can hear the Dayton National Ohio
cash register click on the $1 sign.
You can almost feel the
chariot engraved in the
southwestern wall.
But what you don't notice
nor does he
is that above the door
is a reflection of
a face, my face,
with my staff and halo.
For I am his guardian angel
that watches a man
with winter hair & floor
patterns of leaves.
I am his watcher.

She has entered the inner realms of his world, finding more than meets (so to speak—excuse the pun) the immediate eye. She's added a level of mythical seeing that awakes in us another sense. By noticing that face in the right-hand section of the window above the door, she has conjured a spiritual aspect to this scene that many would never have come to. In such phrases as "winter hair" and "floor patterns of leaves," she evokes stateliness to the scene. With her invention of "the watcher," she has given us a new way to see even such a plain and posed portrait from the world within both the photograph and its "star."

Shelby is another student who, like Matt, had struggled up to this point. In the action-as-metaphor assignment, for instance, she'd written just these three lines, with the rest scribbled out: "I jump like a fox, and then scurry down like a squirrel. I stroll around searching for 'grub.' Then I groom my fur. . . ." For "My mind is like . . . " she got down just these two bits, where others had often written a page:

My mind is like a little pink bouncy ball
ricocheting off a stone wall

My mind is like a bug caught between the
sides of a jar

I suppose her mind might well seem to her like something small bouncing off something vast and unmovable, or stuck sometimes like a bug unable to move between walls of glass, unable to stretch very far, or play in the air the way fireflies do. Metaphor has yet to lift her out.

Play, too, has so far offered Shelby limited possibilities. With the "suppose" assignment, designed as it was to shake the writing out of prosaic ruts, she manages the most perfunctory and mostly meaningless associations like these:

> Suppose you put the blender in the pineapple.
> Suppose a kitten couldn't run.
> Suppose kites jumped.
> Suppose a bowl looked like a saw.
> Suppose your grandma was a building . . .

These lines are not playful. They do little more than fill in the blanks. The only one, later on in her list, that made us laugh read: "Suppose your goal was to become a board." It still causes a chuckle, inadvertently challenging us all to be something more than stiff. How many students in school have, without even knowing it, had such a goal? I have to believe that what kept Shelby going despite all these "failures" was some inner conviction, whether she knew it or not, *not* to become a board. Something kept nagging her to keep trying—and me to urge her on.

What happened next is that we put these historical photographs *in Shelby's hands*. I highlight that phrase because, while it might be too much to say that the "visuality" of those photographs triggered something in her mind, the real answer might be that the "handleability" of those photographs gave her a sense that she could connect with her environment more than anything else we had done. It may also be that she finally got the point—that one could slow down the mind and "just look."

On the day of the Millers's visit she took my suggestion of writing three "supposes," two questions, five details, and two metaphors and tried to get them all in. Taking the photograph in Figure 8.6 as her source, her first version read:

> What if
> . . . the reflections on the new Chevy are foreshadow
> to modern day Zebra Stripes?
> . . . the hydraulic lift uses strength holding life
> up high?
> What if their days have gone bad, but yet they
> keep going, looking intent?
> What if they're old friends from high school
> reuniting, bringing back memories?
> What if they are nothing but kind strangers,
> one helping the other out?

Figure 8.6. Unknown photographer, "Car Lift"

She called me over at this point and asked what I thought of her ideas so far. I have to say I was impressed by the details she put in, by the extra speculation. And she used her first perceptive metaphor in the form of the zebra stripes—she'd actually *seen* the shadows arrayed over the hood of the car. Even her idea that the hydraulic lift held *life* up, rather than just the car, shows an extension she wasn't making use of before. Each line, in fact, was stretching further and reaching for more impact; and she was taking my suggestion of asking "what if?" and making it her own approach to the photograph, rather than just going through the motions as she had before. Still, I told her, she could be more specific. *How* was one man helping the other out? *What* memories might they be sharing? As I moved on to another student, I suggested she draw some arrows under each couplet and add more details before she called the poem done. She added "like when one hit the winning run in during their championship baseball game" to the next to last line, and closed out the poem with two more questions:

What if they're finishing up last minute work
before their wives call them in for dinner?

What if they're friendly Mt. Gileadeans
just doing what they love to do?

Next to "Mt. Gileadeans" she put in parentheses: "I think I just made this word up!"

It's not so much the poem itself as the process Shelby went through in constructing it that most touches me here. For once, there's staying power in her writing. For once, she raised her hand *during* class rather than just writing: "This is really bad" at the bottom and letting it go at that. Had she come to trust herself more—to put down what she thought rather than discounting it beforehand? Had the photograph and the information about Mt. Gilead's past helped? Maybe there was just something more tangible for her now—she didn't have to invent something out of her head, or choose what to write about. Shelby had turned from a tentative, go-through-the-motions writer to a truly speculative one (at least for the course of this poem). Even inventing a term for the people in Mt. Gilead as "Mt. Gileadeans" and reflecting that she "just made this word up" shows a confidence in invention she hadn't exhibited before.

Applying the Lesson on Your Own

Many towns and areas have local historians filled with information about the recent (and not-so-recent) past, and/or local museums a class can visit. As the previous lesson demonstrates, drawing students into this material, either with a guide or with a tour, can be a great way of helping students "step out of the present" and into a much wider range of history. Similarly, entering the photograph through a poem can be a great way to help history become real and more personal.

Lesson 23: The Six-Block Field Trip

All that came before was a kind of warm-up for applying the skills of metaphor, physicality, visuality, and play on their own. My goal, as I told them, was not to turn them into poets, although I look to the flair and detail of their metaphors and lines as clues into the "progress" they are making. All I felt I could give them was the experience of playing with these central poetic concepts as tools they might use for **re-seeing the world around them**, starting with "looking around" the town.

On a Thursday morning, at 7:30 a.m. October 24, we headed downtown—six blocks away. We took the bus, even for such a short distance, since our time was limited and I wanted us to have the whole period for exploration and writing. Once the driver had parked downtown, I set up the assignment, though first we had some catch-up to do. One student, Emma, had written in her journal: "What makes a good poem?" She'd been wondering a lot about it—why certain people get published, whether somebody could just dash something off and it would be okay, but most of all, what made a poem good when it was good? All I could say was: good question! And certainly one it was time to start answering. So at the top of the morning handout I put:

Question: What makes a good poem?

Of course there are many reasons that one poem might stand out more than another. But one reason might be that the poem takes something we see every day and flips it around—helping us see it in a brand new way.

For instance, in the poem "The Builders," Gregory Orr makes us see the beauty of a peaceful field at midnight but as if we could take the moonlight and make a house out of it.

The Builders (for Trisha)

Midnight. The field becomes white stone.
We quarry it. We carry the cut squares
Strapped to our backs.

On the side of a bleak hill,
We build our hut. Windowless,
But filled with light.

Writing a good poem usually means playing with your words in some intriguing way, or with the way you phrase something, or with the entire way you see something.

This led to a heated discussion (well, almost heated) of "The Builders," for, as I might have expected, many did not "get it" at first. Despite my explanation on the page, they had to twist their minds around to see the blocks of moonlight being cut. When they did, it was often an "aha" moment for some of them. Shelby in particular, who in her journal on a similar poem, Jeff Gundy's "Chainsaw Inquiries," had written: "This poem is about all these questions nobody would ever think to ask about a chainsaw. Does *that* make any sense?" All along she'd been struggling to play the game, to see beyond the most prosaic phrasings. But this morning, she woke up briefly with a loud, "Oh, I *get* it!"

Without that "aha," I would suspect, little of what followed would have unfolded. And what's more, we'd have been missing one of the essential aspects of what poems can do: riddle our world (see Lessons 4 and 5). My hope, in introducing such an obscure poem as "The Builders" was to trigger this kind of lyric-seeing in the students, to help them seek another layer of meaning in their poems.

As I began to set up the writing assignment, I realized immediately that I had way too much on the rest of the handout. Besides, it was a bit cold out in the early morning air and threatening to rain. How long would they be able to stay outside, trying out all my choices, before their fingers froze? So I shortened and condensed the whole idea. I had them go out on a little "detail/metaphor/invention" hunt, dividing their papers into three columns, with those headings at the top. They were to look closely, jotting down anything they saw and trying to describe it—in quick notes—in the first column; then try to come up with possible metaphors and similes for what it looked or seemed like in the second; and try out some wild "what ifs" or "supposes" in the third column. Off they went. My last words to them, as they scattered, were: "Try to find different places to watch from—an alley, a corner, up a fire escape . . . or out in the monument which sits in the middle of the intersection."

Many took me up on these suggestions. Amber went up a fire escape that looked over the downtown roofs; Phil decided to be the lone sentry out at the World War I monument in the middle of town. Jenny wandered off to the steps of a church several blocks away. Rachel chose a bench right at the main intersection. I placed myself down in a stairwell right outside the Cornerstone Cafe (selfishly, because it was out of the wind), which forced me to look at the town at eye-level with the street, with stray plants growing out of the concrete steps. Shelby—and I think a few others—actually went *in* the cafe, chose a table, and began to take notes.

This was exactly the kind of gathering and dispersing I was hoping for. It was taking the "let's invent a world" feeling from early childhood and overlaying it across the actual space where most of their parents (and they themselves) banked and drove and shopped. Here they were as high school sophomores, many of them in the process of getting their drivers' licenses, taking on jobs, opening bank accounts, thinking about college, and I was asking them to *play* with the rigid—and seemingly stale—concrete world of a typical Ohio small town on an average, if chilly, Thursday morning in October. Climb up on a roof? Who would do that besides a telephone repairman (or a burglar)? Sit out on the monument? On other days you would be looked at as crazy or dragged in for truancy. Stare at a half-deserted parking lot? What I think was happening was a matter of linking metaphoric play and the physical world to joyfully *toy with the given*, taking time away from ordinary task-thinking into the realm of art-seeing.

After about twenty minutes of taking notes out in the cold morning, we headed back to the heated bus, with wrinkled and rain-dotted notepads in hand. The time was so much more condensed than I'd imagined. Still, we'd been outside . . . and we had rather visceral experiences to go on. The bus became our window, our reflective space, from which to look back on where we'd just been.

I set the rest of the assignment up by quickly surveying the options on the handout, and we read a couple more poems. In this case, I have to say that there was little direct correspondence between the example poems we read and the poems they wrote. Maybe, as with Pattiann Rogers's "Suppose Your Father Was a Redbird," the main point was to be reminded of poetic language—the flash of metaphor, the leaping of a surprising phrase—as one might set up a tonic chord before heading into the playing of a sonata. We heard Mandelstam's "Leningrad," in which he imagines coming back to his old hometown after several years of exile. His nearly surrealistic imagery and wild commands ("this December day / the egg-yolk with the deadly tar beaten into it" and "Open wide. Swallow / the fish-oil from the river lamps of Leningrad") may have just nudged a few of them further into suggestive possibilities.

Many wrote a "here I am and this is what I see" sort of poem. Others were more inventive—taking the point of view of a barber pole, or a parking lot, or a step at the bottom of a church stairway. One might be labeled as a safer approach, the other wilder and riskier. I came to see these as merely two options they carved out of the possibilities I offered them. What's marvelous to me is how many found their own route to the "grail," that of taking in this ordinary space with more engaged eyes.

Rachel took the first approach, a here-I-am poem grounded in sensory imagery:

> I sit on the bench, old and worn,
> surrounded by the tilted pole, the
> half-opened windows, the ding dong
> as the time slips away, the streetlight,
> neglected by day, taken for granted
> at night, the consequences of lazy people,
> beauty, leaves the color of blackberries . . .

Ah, listen to the quiet voice here. This is not Mandelstam leaping up to "swallow the fish-oil from the river-lamps of Leningrad." And that's not the point anyway. Notice instead how keen her sensory images are. The bench is a bit generic, "old and worn," but how? Then she gets gradually more specific and multisensory: while we are noticing that the pole is "tilted," we are simultaneously hearing the sound of the bells. What a careful mixing of imagery, even if she juxtaposed them by accident. Here is what Phillip Wheelwright speaks of with the "diaphoric move" at work, in which the poet unpretentiously places two things side-by-side so that they can suggest resonance rather than overtly making a metaphoric claim. Rachel may just be recording the most telling details from her list. What they do for us as readers, though, is gradually form a scene. To quote a scientist friend of mine (actually, Jill's husband, Tom Grubb, a biologist at Ohio State): she's "arguing from evidence," showing us that she's capable of feeding the tiniest detail into her poem and making us notice.

Brian took the inventive route, picturing himself not just observing his chosen place, a parking lot, but actually *being* the concrete where "the shoots cut through me and stretch towards the sun." Here is his poem:

Confession

I've been worn out.
Years of football and hard shoes
Make potholes in me.
I am all but forgotten.
The shoots cut through me and stretch towards
the sun.
The trash clogs my pores.
Not allowing me to breathe.
But I remember
races down hill,
the victor touching me first.
I was a secret meeting place,
A battleground for wars.
I've seen childhoods
bloom and grow.
And so I shall stay.

I love how he sees below the surface here. He knows that places as empty as this can mean a lot to kids growing up. That's what I'm coming to understand about Brian . . . he's growing up and he's doing well in school, but he's keeping a part of the child-like mind inside him. If nothing else, the poetry seems to be allowing him to do that.

Each poem written that day has something of the fingerprint of the student writer. Tressa comes up with only four lines:

> Wish wash wish wash as the traffic goes by.
> As traffic stops silence fills the air.
> Sidewalks are deserted islands.
> Wish Wash Wish Wash.

And she needed help from Lauren to even come up with that last line! (They made a joke that Lauren should get special credit in the anthology we would be making at the end of our time together.) Even with so small a poem, I can't help smiling, and imagining there's an expansion of her worldview going on. Knowing her, this *is* what she sees: a "paused" moment amid a wide world of energy. If Buson had been our teacher—that wizard of Zen-like attention from sixteenth century Japan—she'd have been his follower perhaps. True, "silence fills the air" is pure cliché. (Or does it? I would have thought that just then other sounds became noticeable.) And yet she prepares us then for the surprise of the sidewalks becoming "deserted islands," with their elongated terrain, almost wish-washed away by the passing vehicles. It's a brief stop, this poem, with a tiny, engaging (and engaged) bit of refreshment.

Lots more was happening, it seems, as the students spread out to watch their town in the early morning mist. Holly, in a move similar to Rachel's, stuck with carefully honed observation, overhearing a man whistling as he walked down the street, "a tune I'd never heard before . . . / . . . so pretty it could almost put you to sleep." Just then the town clock strikes 8 a.m., and "the man looks up. / He looks a while at the peeking tower of the building" and then walks on, continuing his whistling.

Nearby, Ci'Arra was peopling a world hidden under the cracked and peeling paint on a wall, a whole village hiding there, where

> as the waves roll so do their minds
> while they're going cautiously about
> the day. Careful for the rain
> that flees from outside into
> their village, flooding their minds
> with thought . . .

If Rachel is a sensory viewer, Ci'Arra often finds the mythical or fantasy layers. Perhaps the columns upon which they recorded notes guided the styles people chose. While I don't have her original notes, I imagine Ci'Arra jotting down, on the order of our "suppose" game: "Suppose there was a village under the cracked paint, fighting not to drown in the flood of the rain." Like Gregory Orr, she's invested an ordinary scene with potential for inventive meaning.

What I think all our exercises were creating for the students is the *ability to choose their entrance point* for an assignment. Some are more comfortable with viewing things from a distance, as Lauren and Rachel chose. Others need to do a bit of "projective seeing," inventing worlds beneath the cracked paint, hearing the voice of the concrete, breaking up the order of the "normal" banking day, as Sara L. does, with this persona poem in the voice of . . . well, you guess . . .

> Why do I have to turn?
> I'm getting so dizzy
> After all the years I've been here.
> People act like I'm not here
> But I wouldn't look at myself either,
> Seeing my red white & blue skin go
> Up and down, up and down.
> But the people who walk in the
> Door beside me never come
> Back out.
> I see their bodies, just not
> Their heads.

Do you know? It took me a while, too. And then when I saw that she had taken on the voice of the barber pole (Figure 8.7), I saw how much she had internalized that object, making it speak for herself, in a way, much as Gregory Orr has made a mythical space of the midnight field, adapting it to his own internal feeling. In Sara's case, what student does not feel ignored at times? She is often quiet, not making a splash in class. Perhaps here she's found a comrade in arms in the barber pole, turning and turning, taking in the world of heads passing through the door and never returning. . . . This is play and metaphor, and subtle commentary mixed together. Like her fellow writers, she's found a way to *invest herself* in what she sees.

Figure 8.7. Terry Hermsen, "Barber Pole"

Applying the Lesson on Your Own

Each town is unique but areas ripe for investigating and wandering exist any-where. Get outside, take notes, choose your viewpoints, your styles, and your point-of-view . . . and where we are becomes our own in endlessly subtle and individualized ways.

Lesson 24: At the State Park

When Gary Paul Nabham, a naturalist who has written a number of essays and books about children's relationships with the natural environment, reflects on his own growing up in northern Indiana along the shores of Lake Michigan, he comments that: "During my first twelve years of school, I figure that my teachers offered a total of less than six uninterrupted hours in the marvelous natural laboratory at our doorstep: the Indiana Dunes, a hodgepodge of buried forests, quaking bogs, and mountains of sand. Even in a place so well-suited for nature study, my teachers kept us inside classrooms for a thousand hours for every one hour they took us into the field." The same could be said for most of our schools. We need to get out into the terrain and see what happens when we learn to look. America is still out there to be discovered, once we turn away from the easy daze of our TVs. Can we not go to the museums to test our ability to see beyond ourselves and our biases? Can we not go into caves and "take in" environments with which we are unfamiliar?

Here's a wonder: after a rainy early morning when the first class had written about downtown, the sun came out by 10 a.m., in time for me to plan a trip out to Mt. Gilead State Park, a mile out of town, known affectionately by people in town as "State Lakes." Between classes I headed out to check the trail, and by 11 a.m. we were on the road. In this case, not everyone chose to go. A group of boys had decided they were not interested. That's okay. We were a more coherent class without them, for the rest had *chosen* to be here.

I started by having them choose a stone from a pile I'd collected along the dry streambed. Searching for some way to get them involved immediately, at a sensory level, I asked them to "get to know it" as we walked along the trail. Then, for our first stop, I collected their rocks, asking them to close their eyes, and redistributed their stony friends among the group in a random fashion. It's an old environmental education game, the purpose of which is to help us realize that even the smallest stone has its own characteristics, its own unique flavor. As we started to pass the rocks around in a circle, they rather easily were able to find their own again. Perhaps that's not so surprising, yet if they'd seen all those rocks spread across the dried streambed where I collected them, my guess is they'd perceived them as "just a bunch of rocks," without any significantly different characteristics. But if each single *rock* is unique and identifiable by subtle nuances of touch, *what about this place?* There are, after all, state parks all around the country, and most of them have rocks and trees and lakes and streams, and pathways to walk through the woods. I said this to them, asking them to think about their town as well. Don't they know it too by its nuances?

I told them I want to build a case, with their help and through the poems, for the value of the experiment we'd been tackling: making art out of "what's here." Part of my "evidence" for something sinking in is the terrific discussion that followed of two poems about natural areas on the handout I had given them. The first is by the late James Wright, from his wonderful book, *The Branch Will Not Break.*

Milkweed

While I stood here, in the open, lost in myself,
I must have looked a long time
Down the corn rows, beyond grass,
The small house,
White walls, animals lumbering toward the barn.
I look down now. It has all changed.
Whatever it was I lost, whatever I wept for
Was a wild, gentle thing, the small dark eyes
Loving me in secret.
It is here. At the touch of my hand,
The air fills with delicate creatures
From the other world.

Maybe it's good that we started with James Wright. For one thing, it let them know that there are well-known poets out there who grew up in circumstances much like theirs. I told them that he, too, grew up in a small town in Ohio, Martins Ferry, along the river, and that he lived in several other places in his life, including Italy—and Minnesota, where this poem was written—but that he always thought back in his mind to his beginnings, pondering the place he grew up. It seems to me now to be a poem about discovering a different way of seeing.

Without realizing the fact that Wright has seen and touched a milkweed pod, Sara G. said: "It seems that he's talking about himself; something in himself that he lost." And so, without getting it, she's "got it," leaping to the heart of the meaning, even though she misses a key clue. I've noticed that sort of leap-ful meaning in many of the kids. Lauren, for instance, who in her journal said that Gregory Orr's "The Builders" was about "recovering their wonderful love" (well, it is, but it is first of all about building the house of moonlight). They are able to abstract the meaning out, I guess, but I want them to read more slowly, to see *how* the poet got to that important statement, which is, no doubt, the reason for choosing riddle-like poems like "Milkweed" and "The Builders." There are plenty of nature poems that would be quicker to grasp. The riddle slows us down. If we don't understand it right away, we can have a tendency to skip over the possible meanings. But if the riddle makes us *stop*, we can take in the poet's moves, even unconsciously, and perhaps apply them to our own seeing.

We spent so much time with the rocks and the poems (we also looked at Robert Bly's "Summer, 1960, Minnesota") that our time for writing was quickly disappearing. How I wish now that the principal had allowed us to stay the whole afternoon, as originally planned! Quickly, I suggested that they write their own "staring poem," "taking in as much of what you see around you, looking far out, as James Wright does, but then at some point switching and looking closer beside you." Of course I reminded them to weave in metaphor and description to be a tad surprising so that the poem takes on a bit of a riddling form. I forgot, however, to add something I'd planned to: that they imagine they're writing at a different time in their life, not as a member of a class but here for a different reason, after something important has happened or is about to happen. Nevertheless, perhaps because of the slowing down of attention we paid to the stones and the poems, the students brought a rather engaged and inventive spirit to their poems anyway.

David C.'s poem is more a generic "nature poem," though I have to admire him for making the start. He had defied three of his buddies to even come along. Looking back, I think this was the beginning of a change for him, a first step at placing himself in a poem:

> Sitting in the middle of the valley
> on an overhanging log
> Seemingly floating above the earth
> Many colors—green orange yellow brown
> I see the light, flowing to get through
> the trees
> The hillside in front of me
> A disaster of trees twigs leaves and slopes
> It's quiet except for nature playing its own tune
> I stay here, I just take it all in, everything

His friend Sarah K., more than anyone else here, has begun to shape her lines and stanzas (we've seen examples of that already). And so the pacing of her poem is sharper, the nouns sometimes more particular, and the verbs more carefully chosen:

> Place among the trees
> Dead branches torn
> Lying motionless
> Waiting for time
> To pass.

Bitter breeze
nipping the dry air.
Pressing against leaves
as though
waving "goodbye."

Lost among them,
branches, trees, leaves
cold breeze, acorns
lost between life
and death.

Leaning back
against bark
staring down
to where
creatures rustle
guarded by
just this tree

It's nice, when lines spin out this way, how connections can start to happen that were not even originally or consciously intended. Reading her poem back to the class the next week, I wonder aloud if Sarah had thought about the way that acorns indeed are suspended "between life and death," in the way they are no longer part of the large tree they came from and are not yet sprouted (or may never sprout) into new life. She hadn't, but the insight is there for us to gather up anyway. I also like how specific she gets at the end, "guarded by / just this tree." It makes the singularity of trees, in all the wide forest, seem important. I am with her here, leaning back, comfortable in that spot beside the lake.

Finally there's Kelley, who wrote two poems during this time, each twice as long and complex as anybody else's. She said to me later, "I just can't sit and listen to all the talk," so she was writing the first during our discussion, and the second, which I include here, over on a small bridge that spans a part of the trail.

I hear the bridge creak unsteadily
beneath me,
my imagination looks deeper and
spots a troll.
You can dig into our soul,
but be careful,
too deep and you may pay a toll.
Water is shallow.
It's like a painting,
the muddy banks drip softly

into shallow,
still, yet rippling water.
Autumn tinted leaves that
sleep upon the water
look as though they are
small, separate fires
whose flames have silently
faded.
Dull, gray rocks play the
role of headstones.
With my feet dangling aside
the bridge,
it looks & feels as though
I can walk atop the shallow
waves.
I turn as the breeze blows
in,
the other side is completely
different.
The rocks are still entombed
within the dark waters.
But moist blades of fading grass
enclose the rushing waters which
are not so still as the other side
portrays.
Emerging from the lining
are rusted stems,
brightened with the new
blooms of almost
winter berries.

Kelley was struggling at school—and with English in particular. Yet notice how camera-like her eye is, slowly scanning the whole surround, getting a little silly at times (the trolls, the tolls), but mostly bringing out the details of the trees, the rocks, and the deceptive surface of the lake as if it were all on a photographic plate rising up toward her words. In that sense, she reminds me of Chad at Savannah Elementary School, who wrote "Window to the Future" out of a similar exercise. Kelley's interest in poems only started, as I understood it, a few weeks ago, when she refused to read *To Kill a Mockingbird* and Jill suggested she write about the tree outside the window every day, at least to give her something to do. Kelley dropped out of school before the semester was over. Before that, I often wished I could take her anywhere at all—and watch the poems emerge.

Applying the Lesson on Your Own

Not every school has a state park with a lake at the edge of town, but we might have parks and waterways nearby. We can talk all we want in a classroom about experiencing nature and keeping in touch with the basic elements of life—earth, water, fire, and air. But being there? *That's a different matter. Suddenly "being in a place" takes on genuine meaning. And it doesn't have to be in a traditionally "natural" spot. Just somewhere to practice the skills of settling in, noticing, and drawing metaphors and images from what we see and experience. As I pointed out in Lesson 16 on conducting poetry night hikes, nearly everything we do on those evenings in the woods also can be replicated, with some adjustment,* in the daytime *and* in the city.

Lesson 25: Remapping the Town

The next day offered us further time for exploration, even if it was colder and threatening rain. In the second class, I wanted to go downtown, since they'd been at the park the day before, but I didn't want to do quite the same exercise. Instead, I gave them the following map, a dice cube, and told them to go off, pick a place to begin, and start the game, writing two lines in each spot before moving to the next. First, however, I wanted to remind them what a good line was, so, in quick fashion, I asked them to page through our poetry anthology and find a few lines or so (even a single one) that they found striking. This exercise alone gave me confidence that something was sinking in, for the lines they chose had just the kind of power I would be asking them to emulate. They even surprised me by not picking the easy stuff. And just as their lines about "my mind is like" revealed aspects of their personalities, so did the lines they chose. I wrote some of them down afterward.

Sara S., whose own poems were evoking a strong sense of place and rhythmic tension, chose from this poem about growing up in Williamsport, Pennsylvania:

> It was in an empty lot
> Ringed by elms and fir and honeysuckle.

David C. picked out these from a poem of mine, which describes the burning of tent caterpillars discovered in an old orchard, foreshadowing the kind of metaphysical poet he gradually would blossom into:

death-hands as they climbed the black walls
of the flames and fell back in.

Josh, appropriately for him, chose a part of Russell Edson's sting-ingly sarcastic prose poem, "Erasing Amy Loo":

Shut up about Amy Loo. Bring your head over here and I'll erase
Amy Loo out of it.

Ryan, whose family farms 2,000 acres of land, picked these lines about a farming community in the hills of West Virginia:

Dust on the roads, dust
on the sumac

Zack, with his strong Mormon background, chose these lines by Rilke:

I am circling around God, around
the ancient tower

And Kelley, romantic that she is, picked Diane DiPrima:

I am a shadow crossing ice
I am rusting knife in the water
I am pear tree bitten by frost . . .

I had the hope then—and I still do—based on their ease in find-ing these lines, and from our earlier discussion, that if nothing else I might have shown them how to read into a poem, picking evocative lines that might pull them onward. Poetic language is by its nature *not* everyday language. We needed this little opening go-around to remind us of the subtle flair that poets use to help us reenter the world, even in a single line.

So see the game on pages 156–157, constructed intentionally to evoke the sorts of tension-filled lines—lines built upon opposition, sur-prise, and compression—they just picked out and which we'd been ex-perimenting with all semester.

I don't have space to include all the intriguing poems that came out of this game. I worried they would get too scattered, that they wouldn't be able to maintain the wildness they'd put into their "sup-pose" poems. I needn't have. They seemed now to be able to stretch at will, from the rather beautiful nature-based poems of the day before, to these playful, crazily insightful lines from the streets of the town they walk every day. *All despite the fact that it began to sprinkle rain at the exact the moment we stepped off the bus.*

A MAP TO THE TOWN (A POETRY GAME)

A Way to Make a Poem Without Trying to Make a Poem

<u>Directions</u>: For each spot, do what the directions say, then write two lines or so as if they were part of a poem you were making.

1. Start somewhere no one else is (where you can't see other class members).

   Jot down ten nouns from what you see—each with a strong sound of B, D, G, K, P, or T.

   Then write two strong lines of poetry using two of those words in each line, paying attention to how your *second line* plays against your first, and extending it or contrasting with it in a way that catches us off guard.

2. Cross a street (carefully!) and find a new place to sit.

   Jot down four unusual pairs of "opposites"
   (example: What if **window** were the opposite of **sky**?)

   Write two lines using those opposites, such as:
       "The window blurs its own thoughts on purpose"
       "The sky peels apart the clouds."

3. From that same spot, pick someone you can see (not a fellow student) or imagine someone—even someone in a car.

   Write two or four lines that begin, "All day, he . . ." or "All day, she . . ."

4. Stay in that spot, or find some place no more than 10 steps away. Find something small around you—smaller than a breadbox or smaller than your hand.

   Look at it for at least two minutes, noticing little things about it.

   Write two or four "impossible questions" about it—thinking of it as if it were human or had a point of view and feelings of its own . . .
       As in: "Does the stoplight at night wish to vanish into a dozen shells beneath the lake?"

   Don't worry about making sense—just make your questions create interesting pictures and possibilities.

5. Walk no more than one block in either direction. Stop and look around. Throw the die you were given—or pick a number in your head between 1 and 6, looking in the direction the number below gives you:

   1 = up / 2 = down / 3 = in front of you /
   4 = behind you / 5 = to the right / 6 = to the left

Take something you see and write two lines that begin,

"Everybody knows . . ."

Don't stay necessarily in the realm of reality. Invent. Be playful. Yet be specific. As in:

"Everybody knows the bricks were once able to listen . . ."

6. Take two lines that you wrote already and write the opposite of what they say.

7. Find a spot and sit down. Write two lines from the point of view of someone who left Mt. Gilead 20 years ago.

8. Walk somewhere zigzag from where you are. Stop and look around. Find something around you that is the same color as something you have on.

Using that color (and/or that thing) as a starting place, write two lines that begin, "I never . . ." or, "I once . . ."

9. Write two lines that are a "creative lie."

10. Without turning your head, from the side of your eye (your peripheral vision) find a source of light. Look at it, or walk closely up to it.

Write two to four lines that begin, "The light is like . . ." or "The light is . . ."

NOW:

Sit down somewhere close by and spin your various lines into a single poem, adding or subtracting (dividing and recombining) as needed.

You might think of it as just a series of "images from Mt. Gilead," or you might try imagining that they all come from the point of view of one person or thing you saw during the "game."

Here are just three examples to get the idea of what they were able to construct out of seemingly random phrases. Most people didn't have time to do that final stage of weaving the lines together—it was Friday after all—so we let the groupings stand on their own. Here, to begin, is Erin's. Note how she starts with the most mundane of observations (people and dentists make up a town as much as the bricks and pavement) and opens suddenly wider. It's as if the first stanzas provided her with a bit of "ground" upon which she can build a much wilder structure:

Mt. Gilead

1
As the pavement and bricks make up this town
The people and dentists help it too

2
The music plays softly in small novelty shops
As rain hits the ground as if it were angry
The air conditioner wrrrs to try to cool down
The chair acts as if it were a resting place

3
All the day, he walks to his job
All the day, he dreams about rain

4
If a door knob were not to open a door,
Would people still eat bananas?

5
If silver wasn't a color, would unicorns
Still dance on otter's brains?

6
Everybody knows the door will open
To a field of dreams
Everybody knows that trucks dream
About eating chicken teriyaki

7
He never attempts to walk around
The rain never comes in his dreams

8
The cozy little bustling town makes me
Think of my old home
As the traffic clogs the busy one-way streets
I remember the small streets of Mt. Gilead

—Erin

I love the oppositional combinations that are starting to happen here. I'm in a quite "real" place—with dentists and truck drivers, novelty shops and air conditioners—which comprises one side of Mt. Gilead. And then, as if the directions to the game sprung loose a series of trap-doors underneath her more prosaic lines, a new tune begins to play across her keyboard: a man dreams all day about rain, doorknobs threaten *not* to open, trucks have culinary desires, the rain reverses and refuses to return to his dreams. We are walking the line Susan Stewart defines in her book *Nonsense*, where what makes sense is continually in negotiation with what does not.

Josh's contribution has something of that same natural combining power, if more closely observed wackiness:

> 1
> The pebble-basined pole stood fast in the belly of the earth
> Slowly the bug had reached its power line
>
> 2
> What if money were opposite the business that made it?
> What if signs and their meanings had no bond?
>
> 3
> All day she drives around, not know where around is
>
> 4
> Does this number want to be more or less than a stuck-fast
> shape will allow it?
>
> 5
> Everyone knows that the true color of stop is blue
> Everyone knows that stop has been cursed
>
> 6
> The pebble-covered pole leans over from arthritis
>
> 7
> The small insignificant ignorance of that place
> It pulled the shades everyone and even the blind
> could see better
>
> 8
> Did you know, it's true, only small things fall
> and the large have to hold them up

As he's shown in other assignments, Josh is able to merge the mythical and the realistic in paired lines that open up both sides of the world. His "pebble-basined pole" is a very *real* pole to me, but as it stands fast in the "belly of the earth," it takes on more than mundane meanings. And when he pairs it with the bug as it "slowly reach[es] its destination," the whole world of the small takes on a richness that our "quick sight" approach to a town like Mt. Gilead is bound to miss. Perhaps by breaking his poem into tiny surreal supposes, Josh creates a composite picture of the place that is stronger than if he had written a more "regular" poem.

Finally, and perhaps most surprisingly, there's Ashley S.'s poem, which she took time to revise into something of a whole. Reading it over, I recalled her single line of a few weeks before, "My mind is like a flower, alive," and marveled at the way that first stab at tensive language grew into this swirl of surprise.

> What if pavement was the opposite of people?
> Would it open the doors of bricks?
> Everybody knows the bricks can sing and dance.
> And whisper among themselves.
> And the man that goes through the doors
> of bricks—
> Who is he?
> All day he pushes a cart full of pieces of
> cardboard.
> All day he speaks Chinese.
> The bug beneath his foot,
> what does it dream about?
> Popcorn and moss?
> Does it, was it, could it be one of us,
> and does it have to worry about being
> squished beneath moving towers?
> The light is like beautiful teardrops . . .

Notice how wide-ranging and sensory Ashley's references and camera angles have become. She's gained a much more dramatic and flexible **engagement with the world,** now focusing on the bricks, adding music to vision, zeroing in on a man passing through a door, and then zooming even closer to the bug beneath his feet. She even gives us two possible dreams for that bug and then shifts back to a much grander view—of two moving towers (which could be at one and the same time our legs *and* the World Trade Center), and the light shedding its tears over all. To "engage" the world this way, I will always hope, is a way of taking the ordinary and seeing the riches inside.

Applying the Lesson on Your Own

Forests and state parks may be hard to reach, but local shopping areas and downtowns are everywhere. Make sure the students are safe crossing streets, etc., and then turn them loose with the worksheet (or a variation) and have them launch into an invented way of "taking in the world." It helps if the students have had some experience with "line-weaving" before—as in our previous "supposing" exercise or the writing from paintings exercise in Lesson 28—just so they can concentrate on making fiercely original connections here.

Lesson 26: Writing at Kroger

As it turns out, one of my contingency plans for the field trips provided a nice change of pace for the final assignment of our two days "out on the town." Not knowing what the weather would be like in this third week of October, I thought we might need a place to go inside should it be rainy or cold. At 7:30 Friday morning it was both, so we headed off to Kroger, where I'd gotten permission for the kids to wander the store, hunting up poems along the aisles of flashy, tempting packaging and the mounds of Californian and Chilean produce.

Only later did I think of the contrast this assignment made with the other field trips. For here we were, writing, in a way, about visual culture, or at least about the packaging that surrounds our daily sustenance. Grocery stores in America are not all about filling necessities, or even mainly. They are cultural events that buy into a visual and visceral wash of consumption, in which what something looks like on the package often has much more to do with why we like it than what is necessarily in the box.

The store's location is telling: it sits as the head-pin of Mt. Gilead's version of a strip mall, set back from the road surrounded by a parking lot as large as a good-sized lake, with a chain clothing store on its west side and a Radio Shack, McDonald's, and video store across the street—all the most basic "signs" of the national, commercial culture eating its way into the traditional fabric of the cozy "old town" just eight or so blocks away. By coming here, in a way, we actually had left Mt. Gilead and entered America, the store looking like every other chain grocery anywhere else.

Of course the kids were thinking none of this. I'd even guess that this world is closer to the world they inhabit most of the time. They don't, for the most part, wander downtown, poking down alleys, or propping up benches, nor do they spend endless hours at the state park. They *do* make nearly daily trips to the store, as well as consuming the endless food ads on TV, or directly out of the box. It was clear, from the moment we walked in, they felt comfortable here. And so, I'm glad we gave them this chance to see what poetry has to say in such a place. When they got off the bus, it felt like a party. I joined in and went with the flow.

But first—of course—we paused to set up the assignment, making again the bus our classroom. I had come up with ten ideas for writing in this place, but we only had time for two. We read Pablo Neruda's "Ode to Watermelon," a fun poem to start off with, with its burgeoning imagery for this "tree of intense summer," this "jewel box of water . . . warehouse / of profundity, moon / on earth!" whose

> hemispheres open
> showing a flag
> of green, white, red,
> that dissolves into
> wild rivers, sugar, delight!

They'd seldom seen metaphor used so profusely before, at least in this half-mocking way, exaggerating on purpose what we all love but may never have thought of praising so wildly. And so it seems like a liberating poem. For a change, instead of having to be serious, it invited us to be extravagant in what we love. I suggested the students might try the same, writing odes to cheese or celery, Froot Loops or Snickers, and stuffing the poem with as many wild metaphors as they could, but in their exaggeration trying to find something "true" in the food itself.

For a second, shorter idea, I took as a model William Carlos Williams's well-known poem, written they say as a note left for his wife on the kitchen table before heading off to his office in Patterson, N.J., where for most of his adult life he was a family physician. I tell them this because, just as we are making poetry out of the everyday world around us, Williams made poems out of people he saw at the bus stop, or visions outside the hospital window, or what he ate for breakfast, as in this one, where he apologies for eating the plums his wife had been "saving/for breakfast." You can find his poem in nearly any anthology of American poetry from the twentieth century—or in his selected poems.

Justifiably famous as one of the sweetest (excuse the pun), most moving poems ever written in America, it captures a magic within the ordinary—and a cadence within daily speech—that is nearly meditative, focused as it is on the simplicity of pure, if somewhat forbidden, enjoyment. So I suggested that, along with an "ode to cheese" poem, they "write a poem as if it were a note you might leave on some shelf in the store for someone to find later (or else a poem-as-a-note you might leave on the kitchen table), apologizing for something you're not quite really sorry for.

Some of their poems are similarly indulgent and "sinful":

Ode to Reese's Peanut-Butter

Brown creamy peanut butter
rich with a nutty chocolate taste
smoothly plastered over a warm
piece of bread . . . mmm . . .

Ode to the Bakery

Friendly old ladies
serving hungry girls
giving extra rolls to please

—Shelby

It was Shelby's short poems that clued me in to their comfort in this somewhat artificial world. Particularly in this second poem, she reveals a sense of community and camaraderie not seen in the downtown poems, in which the dominant sign of life is traffic and "sidewalks [are] desert islands." From her love of the food, she has, in these tiny poems, produced gems of unfettered enjoyment, crystallized into tight, suggestive language.

Ben V.'s poetry also came to life in this place. Is it a kind of **play** that the food poems allowed him—and others—to indulge in? Here's his "Ode to Pudding":

Oh it is me, that awful stealer of
appetites.
That mischievous thief, innocence.
I am a wonderful thick snack.
I am wrapped in colorful paper to catch your eye.
People dream of swimming in pools of me.
A pack of 4?
Oh, just one more!

The pack is through,
Such a lonely spoon . . .

Tellingly, when we read this out loud in class the next week, people nearly applauded Ben's last line. It was perhaps, as for Shelby, his passage into letting the poetry speak in *his* voice.

The last lines took on more importance now, no doubt under the influence of Williams's zinger of a final stanza—"Forgive me/they were delicious/so sweet/and so cold." Without belaboring it, they seemed to have come to *know* how essential it was to have that last line "click shut":

Note

I ask for your
forgiveness,
I have taken
the Captain Crunch

I'm sorry but the
brightness of the yellow
box drove me to it.

Surely you would
have done the same
thing if you had
skipped breakfast

—Liz

Sometimes a writer would stumble on an unexpected emotional, even existential, tone, as in Brenna's following poem about those little salty fish crackers known as . . .

Fisheys

I was birthed
into a heat
many on either
side
There was but
a slight
indent
upon my
face
different flavors
yet all
the same
I see my
fate
I enter the
mouth of death
only to swim
in the sea
of me

—Brenna

Is it too much to consider this poem a wry comment on consumption, or a meditation on "the other" that we become? Probably. What the students gained in our little jaunt to the grocery was something of the value of hyperbole and irony, and of choosing the right tone to fit your subject. For Brenna, too, this day was the first time that her poems took on this kind of pacing . . . a play with line breaks that led to a much finer tuned melody within. Somehow the **style** they found to respond to the food aisles of Kroger fit—quite intuitively—that place itself.

Even Kelley is able to transform her normally elegiac voice to explore new territories of tone in her poem called:

Sorry

I know your project was due,
I'm sorry,
I took the Twizlers that
Supported your house.
I'm sorry,
I chewed the Marshmallows
That hung as your clouds.
I'm sorry,
I gummed down the gummi bears
That once stood as your family.
I'm sorry,
I snatched the candy corns that
The bad boy wore as a dunce cap.
I'm sorry,
I scarfed down the Pez that
Were your once-burning candles
On your miniature dining table.
But the thing I'm sorry for most of all
Is that I'm not even sorry.
Your family was delicious,
Everything and all.

Applying the Lesson on Your Own

A word of caution: I'd only try this type of an excursion with a class you know well and with students you could trust to wander food aisles and actually get some writing done.

And a word of hope: With the right class, the very freedom this exercise requires, coupled with their ability to handle it, can be a test of how well a class has grasped the skills of poetry. If they can successfully find ways to try out their voice here, where distractions wait around every corner, they may well have the skills to apply it anywhere.

9 Engaged Perception

Lesson 27: Visions from *The Crucible*

Images are at work at all levels of human thought and communication, from the vaguest sense-impression to the most elaborate mathematical formula, from the largely pictorial image in a painting or photograph to the more verbal imagery of poetry and speech. As W. J. T. Mitchell has said, in a reference quoted earlier, an image operates "something like a figure on the stage of history," carrying meanings that are both visual and verbal—and that there is a constant, complex "interplay" between the two, over time, sometimes with one dominating, sometimes with the other (*Iconology*, 8–9). My final four sessions with the students dealt with building links between visual imagery and its relationship to the sorts of verbal imagery they'd been making such subtle use of in their poetry so far.

We began with exploring the imagery in a literary text—Arthur Miller's well-known play, *The Crucible*. Not planning to connect this particular reading into our activities, I was sitting in class on the Tuesday after our two days writing around the town of Mt. Gilead, just to "settle back in" to knowing them as a class in their normal environment. I couldn't resist being pulled under the spell of Arthur Miller's scheme.

The very title of the play offers itself up for consideration: Is it an image or a metaphor? Is it effective? What is it trying to convey? Just as the phrase "to kill a mockingbird" only loosely pertains to the full meaning of Harper Lee's book and yet holds our attention enigmatically, the way a good proverb does, so the image of "the crucible" is more of a condensed and elusive image for the play, moving several directions at once.

So on Thursday I began our session by asking *them* to read back their poems from the field trips. So far, I'd been reading their poems back to them, something I enjoyed doing and which I felt gave the writers a chance to experience what they had written from a fresh view. But it was time for them to take more ownership. From that opening, we moved to *The Crucible* and I hinted at some of the ideas about imagery touched on earlier. Images, I suggested, were often incredibly powerful, just as someone can present a "cool" image in school or at an office and carry a lot more respect than someone with the same ideas and knowledge who does not "read" cool. I gave them the example of Herb E. Smith, a filmmaker from Kentucky who had visited my college class the previous week to show his documentary on the history of the "hill-billy" image and its effect on the people who grow up in Appalachia. I told them of one reference the film made to a newspaper columnist in New York around 1912 who argued against strict laws prohibiting child labor on the grounds that working in factories would lure the mountain children away from what he saw as the lazy habits of their elders. He had an "image" in his mind of "Appalachian = lazy," I suggested, which he proceeded to invoke in his readers to argue for a cause. I wondered aloud how often *"image* ➔ leads to ➔ *action"* this way.

For an example from the play, I asked them to turn to pages 24 and 25. Here, three characters "debate" the significance of the recent odd experiences of some of the girls in town, one of whom, Ruth Putnam, has fallen into a kind of half-coma, while others have been found dancing in the woods. Rebecca Nurse, one of the oldest women in town and well-respected for her wisdom and her kind heart, says:

> I have eleven children, and I am twenty-six times a grandma, and I have seen them all through their silly seasons, and when it come on them they will run the Devil bowlegged keeping up with their mischief. I think she'll wake when she tires of it. A child's spirit is like a child, you can never catch it by running after it; you must stand still, and, for love, it will soon itself come back.

Stunning, isn't it, how this is nearly entirely hinged on metaphoric reasoning and assumption? (It is, to my knowledge, nearly parallel to Dr. Benjamin Spock's philosophy of childrearing, so popular at the time Miller wrote his play, in 1952.) Consider "silly season," for instance. This is a marvelously playful image for picturing what we call "a phase"—as in "this phase will pass." To her mind, and Spock's, children should be allowed to be explore their emotions. A rather liberal, twentieth-century viewpoint for those Puritan times, I would think, but wise nonetheless.

Mrs. Putnam, her daughter lying there, cannot be so calm. "This is no silly season, Rebecca," she demands. Rather, "my Ruth is bewildered," adding as evidence of the severity, "she cannot eat." Either she's experiencing a silly season or she's desperately bewildered—ah, there hinges the choices this Puritan society will make. But the arguments get fiercer as these two pages unfold. Mr. Putnam has talked the town's minister into calling in a professional witch hunter to investigate. This action is seen by John Proctor, the protagonist of the play, as using the rumors of witchcraft to secure a stronger hold on the Salem congregation, and he claims, "This society will not be a bag to swing around your head, Mr. Putnam."

So we get yet a third turn-of-the-phrase to describe what is going on. Rebecca's as a silly season of adolescent pranks, Mrs. Putnam's as a bewilderment (leading to an image of witchcraft), and Proctor's interpretation of the whole event being *used* (as a bag swung around Putnam's head) for political control. In less than two pages, the argument will ricochet between these competing voices until Mrs. Putnam adds a fourth image, born out of her loss of several children in childbirth and infancy, and leading her to a conviction that something evil is at work: "You think it God's work that you should never lose a child, nor grandchild either, and I bury all but one? There are wheels within wheels in this village and fires within fires!"

To consider the power of her image, I suggested to the class: Try walking down the street of your priorly peaceful Salem village, thinking "wheels within wheels and fires within fires" and not feel some cause for action.

Okay, enough background. It was time to tackle using imagery on our own in response to the play, which is something quite different than finding the imagery within it, for I didn't want to have them merely "write a moment" in the play. We'd already done that. I wanted them to try out "living imagery" in response to the play. We took a glance at a couple of poems that evoke powerful images and ones that don't so much dabble in metaphor as open up a marvelous image for us to dwell in, one of which was Denise Levertov's "Blue Africa." In it, the poet conjures, in the midst of a busy intersection, an image where she sees

> . . . elephants cast
> a blue river of shadows

and hears

> a quiet in Africa,
> hum without menace.

She asks that we remember,

> they are there
> now.
> Each in turn
> enters the river of blue.

So here the pattern emerges again, in a kind of poetic argument: Image (elephants) → leading to metaphor (a quiet, a hum without menace, symbol of peace) → encouraging action (in this case, remembrance).

I'm beginning to think, I told them, that we inevitably live our images, hidden as they usually are, like that mirage of elephants caught in New York City traffic.

What I asked the students to do was this: to write in the voice of one of the characters in the play, but put them in some moment *outside* of the story, perhaps at a point not mentioned in the action itself, one made up by the student or loosely mentioned on stage but not portrayed. And then to "suppose" the character has had a vision or a dream. "What would that dream or vision be?" I asked. "Spell it out in the form of a poem."

Here's one from Brenna, latching on to the frightening physical image of the "poppet," toy dolls the accusing girls would use to indicate someone was attacking them "in effigy" by sticking sewing needles in the dolls themselves and claiming someone else (such as Elizabeth Proctor) had done it:

The Poppet

The doll
arms & legs so frail
so light as a
feather

Toss her
and she floats
but only on
the peace
and tranquility
of the world

Anger fills the room
the floating now
is like the fast
dive from a
plane

Sharp and glistening
on the floor
I fall—hard
It pierces me

        —Brenna

Corky took on a more minor character (to his credit), imagining Giles Corey's point of view as he is being buried in stones. Ending his poem (and Giles's life) with the line, "knowing that the weight of the law had done me in," I believe Corky is perhaps quite cognizant of the double-meaning in his phrase. The "weight of the law," in this case, is an ironical image. It destroys lives, rather than protecting them.

Heather also is able to step outside the main circle of characters, choosing Tituba, the only nonwhite in the play, a slave from the West Indies accused of leading the girls into dangerous liaisons in the forest:

> They come to me for help.
> Ancient spirits speak,
> Connecting with another world.
> In wispy shades of white
> They dance with the trees,
> Humming a mysterious melody.
> One which only I understand.
> These unchained souls lend their help,
> But the world doesn't want them.

Let's look back at this tiny, deceptive gem of a poem. I like, for starters, how open it is. Not judgmental of Tituba, and not buying into all the assumed tones. The dancing is not a "silly season," and not "the fires of hell." Rather, it connects the girls "with another world"—a different social frame, perhaps—one where the body is not such a threat, or a different spiritual realm, one more in touch with the earth. They "dance with the trees," as Heather puts it; *with* the trees, not just among the trees. That's a nice, subtle twist. If it's not unusual enough for a blonde-haired, sixteen-year-old girl— the homecoming queen of her class a month ago—to take on so effectively the viewpoint of an old, black conjuring woman from the West Indies four hundred years ago, let's consider the following poem by Brian, a sixteen-year-old lineman on the football team. Yes, he's already chosen to pull off writing from the point of view of a parking lot downtown, and then from the point of view of the villain (Mr. Ewell) as he tries to murder Atticus Finch's children. Now he takes on the point of view of a woman, Elizabeth Proctor, in jail (a scene not shown in the story), dreaming "her prince will come." Watch how subtly he makes his moves, drawing us into her psyche:

> The dirt is rusting,
> But light
> shoots like an
> arrow through it.
> The wall breaks
> down.
> There he stands,
> his head like
> a torch,
> his body,
> the sun.
> He reaches
> for me,
> I for him.
> We touch
> and I feel
> silk and water,

yet feel nothing.
He raises his glamorous wings
and sails on the
moonlight,
the wall fixes
itself,
but I am
not afraid,
for I have
the light in
me.

When I read this poem back to the class the next day, Jill broke into tears
(she has a habit of doing that when poems move her), for she realized,
she said, Brian was talking not just of an angel, perhaps healing her
spirit, or preparing to take her to heaven, but of her husband, John Proc-
tor, restoring their strained marriage.

As with Heather's poem, Brian's vision here is more sophisticated
and clever than it first seems. It is, in fact, **interpretation at work**; mean-
ing-making **in the form of image-making.** How else to "get inside
Elizabeth's head" this way? In an essay? Perhaps. Or not. Even there
he would have had to resort to this sort of imagery to link John and the
angel, her earthly renewal and her heavenly salvation.

Imagery is powerful stuff—and perhaps worth separating from
metaphor, at least at times. I'm convinced much more could be done
with students making use of dreams and visions in creating images that
help us visualize a character's situation or personality in a novel or play.

Applying the Lesson on Your Own

Though The Crucible *is particularly well suited to an investigation of imag-
ery, many other novels and plays would be as well. In a sequence of lessons,
such as what we conducted over the course of the semester, it would be instruc-
tive to try a "metaphor-based" and/or an "enter the moment" exercise for writ-
ing poems about one book, as we did with* To Kill a Mockingbird, *and to then
do an "image-based" and/or "writing outside the novel" exercise for another.
Consciously reflecting on the difference can be an exciting way of investigat-
ing how images work in society at large.*

Lesson 28: A Game for Writing about Visual Art

Maybe through all this talk about imagery, something happened to Shelby's attitude in class. Maybe it was something in her unconscious. A week or so after the field trips around town, she came up to the front of the room before class. Students were milling around in the usual way, off-handedly talking with Mrs. Grubb, or catching up with friends from the other side of the room. She seemed to want to tell Mrs. Grubb something important, but Jill being busy, she turned to me and said, "Oh, I might as well tell you, since you're in it." "In what?" I said. "My dream. You were the bus driver." And she proceeded in her flustered way to relay to me her dream from the weekend (I asked her afterward to write it down). She called it:

Shelby's Dream

We were going on a field trip to write poems about old buildings, and I was trying to direct you (the bus driver) to my church. Well I kind of got us lost, and we ended up on this road (near Galion) that my family and I take to get to my Grandparents' house. But at the intersection that we were at, there were two old buildings—one on each side of the road.

Well my parents were on the bus, and they said that they owned this "building/house" (which looked like an old schoolhouse), so my parents took me in it and showed me around. And the inside was a mixture of my aunt's house and an old Victorian house. So I decided to go around by myself, and I managed to get downstairs and it was HUGE! There were like 50 "great rooms" and this bar (which I don't know why it would be there b/c my parents don't really drink) and all this other cool stuff. Oh, and then when I went out to see the pool, the outside wasn't a schoolhouse, it was what a normal huge house would look like. (Yeah, and I don't know what happened to you and Mrs. Grubb and the rest of the class.)

I was stunned—and pleased. I told Shelby it seemed very Jungian, of course having to describe who Carl Jung was. I said maybe she'd run into him if she ever took psychology—and that his theory of the collective unconscious might have something to say about her dream. I described his dream of seeing ancient Roman soldiers marching through his house, only to find out later that the house was built right on top of what used to be an old Roman highway. Here's what she wrote on the other side of her dream page:

So here are some possible "reasons" why I had this dream:
1. I'm a big weirdo.
2. We have a pool (there was a pool in the dream—although it was like 10× mine)—and we are redoing one of our living rooms and adding on to our kitchen, garage, dining room and possibly adding a "mud room" . . . So maybe this is how I want our house to turn out like?—I don't know.
3. What the guy you were talking about said . . . I think the answer is #1. :)

Whatever the "reason" she had this dream, something amazing had just happened; maybe several things. First of all, she'd decided to trust me enough to tell it to me, even if I was her second choice for an audience. Second, she'd taken the time to write it down in some detail— way more detail, and much more interesting and direct detail, than she has in any of her poems (she'd told me she'd do it in math class, because she never pays attention there anyway). Third, maybe all our talk about there being "something under the surface" in the area they lived in was sinking in. Last, despite all her struggles with poetry, it indicates that more was going on than I knew. The poems that emerged from this next assignment—for Shelby and for a good deal of the others—showed something of the unconscious mind at work.

Continuing with our investigation of images, on Friday I gave the students the following thoughts.

What Do Images Do?

1. Images are not irrelevant. They influence us, often outside of our conscious thought.

2. They can: guide or motivate us
    sometimes force us to choose
    clarify things for us
    sometimes deceive us
    make us see things we might have missed
    divide us from, or unite us with others
    spark us awake
    define us (or define others for us)
    give us meaning

3. They are not strictly from the eyes—they can arise from a sound, a smell, or a song.

4. They can be either very personal or very political.

I suggested that one thing perhaps poetry and art can do is give us a kind of practice in responding to other people's images and creating images of our own.

As an example, we considered the following poem by Wislawa Szymborska. I told them that Szymborska won the Nobel Prize a few years ago, and that a good deal of her poetry was written during Communist rule in Poland, where one had to keep the message a little hidden, lest the authorities detect some criticism of the state. I also mentioned that in Europe final exams can be quite grueling.

Bruegel's Two Monkeys

This is what I see in my dreams about final exams:
two monkeys, chained to the floor, sit on the windowsill,
the sky behind them flutters,
the sea is taking its bath,

The exam is History of Mankind.
I stammer and hedge.

One monkey stares and listens with mocking disdain,
the other seems to be dreaming away—
but when it's clear I don't know what to say
he prompts me with the gentle
clinking of his chain.

Not very descriptive, nor strictly interpretative, it's a poem about the poet making a personal, playful connection with the painting, adding her own life experience into it. Nevertheless, it's important to note, Szymborska doesn't ignore what's there. She simply condenses it into terse, effective language and then sets it into a fresh context. In one grand gesture, she has made the painting metaphoric and able to speak to us in a brand new way. Does she deny history or Bruegel's original context? I think not, for who are these monkeys? In Bruegel's time they would have been importees from the exotic lands the Dutch were then trading with, living symbols of wealth and collection. And for Szymborska, four hundred years later, quite accurate symbols for the chained elements in the history of mankind.

We talked about the subtle use of metaphor in the poem—the sea taking its bath, the sky fluttering—but what about those two monkeys? What did the students make of their role, in the painting or the poem? David Fuller pointed out that one seems to be in a daydream . . . and that the writer is too, daydreaming in the midst of an exam. Jill interjected that it is also the daydreaming monkey, not the one who looks with mocking disdain, who prompts her with the clinking of his chain. (I love, by the way, that last line making the painting take on an aural quality—a good example of a multisensory image.) I asked, "What is the significance of the final exam being the History of Mankind?" And Zack then hit on the idea that maybe we *think* we're advancing, developing new technologies all the time, but we have to remind ourselves of our history and our limitations. Coming from this science-fiction-oriented computer whiz, that's a telling statement.

Now it was time for writing. I told them I was going to show them a series of eight or so slides from paintings. I wanted them to quickly compose two or so lines as if they were starting a longer poem about the piece, or as if those lines came from the middle of a longer poem. I suggested they do something of the following, varying their approach for each slide:

- Pretend the painting is a memory of yours;
- Imagine it as a dream you once had;
- Take the point of view of a small object in the work;
- Create a metaphor from what you see . . . etc.

At this point I trusted that they knew their own voices well enough to "write from intuition," leaping to connections that they don't have to consciously think out. They wouldn't have time anyway—and that (I don't tell them) is part of the point, to circumvent analysis in order to get directly to imagery.

The sweet, utterly nonprosaic, leaping lines that resulted are the product of our weeks working with playful, physicalized metaphor—but also of our engagement with the compelling visual work before us. Intriguingly, several of the students who had not shown much flair before began at this point to shine. Garrison, for instance, came up with these responses:

For Magritte's "The Voice of the Blood" (Figure 9.1 on p. 176):

I sit perched above the valley
and ask myself, does the river ever end?

For Van Gogh's "The Starry Night" (Figure 9.2 on p. 178):

It's like the sky is swirling together with the town,
as if everything were being combined into "one."

For Jerry Uelsmann's untitled photograph (Figure 9.3 on p. 179):

It is as if a bird, floating among the clouds,
with its wings spreading further with time.

And for Magritte's painting of candles on a beach (Figure 9.4 on p. 180):

It is as a nightcrawler, coming out onto the wet grass,
enjoying itself, just breathing.

Figure 9.1. René Magritte, "The Voice of the Blood"

In this case, it's in the middle two stanzas where Garrison at last begins to dig his way into metaphor. Previously, his best poem so far was a straightforward description of his early football days—and not a metaphor in sight. Here you can begin to feel the night sky swirling into one (a fresh take on the picture). And the Uelsmann lines, if vaguer, do a fine job of opening up the photograph for me. If I read Garrision's imagery right, the house is the bird here and the walls are its wings. That too is fresh for me—it puts the house up in the sky, rather than bringing the sky down. Might one say that here Garrison has learned to *play* with how he sees the world, if just a little bit?

It is Emma, though, who outshone us all—or should I say "out-myths" us? As she had shown before, she seems to thrive on this sort of high-energy condensation of ideas into the space of two lines. For now, consider what she wrote about the first Magritte:

> What if the house were painted pink? Would the caterpillars still crawl to their windows?

Here, like Szymborksa, Emma has lifted the painting to new meaning by adding something *not* there into it. Color and speculation have taken on a fairy-tale feeling. The same for her response to Van Gogh:

> The black shadow gathered his belongings and traveled out of the classroom into the starry night.

Using personification, Emma has given the night back its story. She's made the poem into a tiny mystery, where the shadow has gone to infuse the sky with his "belongings."

And look what she does with the Uelsmann, once again investing it with a tiny story and with motion:

> The owl's gaze rested upon the baby mouse. As he swooped down from the clouds he grasped his prey, scurrying across the mantle.

But of course! If the roof is open, what's to prevent an owl from continuing its hunt right into the mouse's hiding place?

After just six slides, I asked them to write their best lines on slips of paper and put them in piles corresponding to the paintings they were written about. Pairs of students then took those lines and wove them into single poem, cutting words where needed, and sometimes dividing and recombining the lines to make for more surprise or better flow. One example should convey the effect. Here is what Sarah K. and Sara G. constructed for "The Starry Night":

Figure 9.2. Vincent Van Gogh, "The Starry Night"

The stars glisten like a thousand diamonds
in the night sky
while below, the village soundly sleeps.

The sky crashes to the ground,
like a tidal wave.

The moon looks me in the eye,
almost as if he knows me.

The jagged brown thing seems like a hand
reaching out for guidance. But the wind silently carries
away the pleas. It is as if the wind were God ignoring you.

The church's steeple
(needle sharp)
pierces the night sky.

The games here represent "ways into" the paintings, just as some
art historians recently have suggested that paintings offer up a chal-
lenge that must be met, in a playful way; just as the games we played
downtown shook us out of our normal ways of approaching any scene.

Figure 9.3. Jerry Uelsmann, "Untitled"

Figure 9.4. René Magritte, "La Méditation"

Yes, working from surreal pieces gave certain students a head start—especially those who tend to take things literally anyway. There's a sense of permission the painting gives such students: "Okay, see, it's okay to be a little weird . . . it can even be beautiful, just look at me."

If we are after giving students the means to develop more engaged worldviews, these lessons in "quick-writing" about paintings tell us that an immediate, intuitive response, built on metaphor and projection, can teach us to *be less distant*, to avoid the pitfalls of abstraction (somewhat), and to participate in one's own perceptions as on a field of play.

Applying the Lesson on Your Own

This game easily inserts itself into any stage of a poetry-writing sequence, as it teaches a close attention to the making of lines, as well as the opportunity to "instantly revise" sequences of lines into larger poems. Along with sequencing slides, it's just as easy to put together a PowerPoint of images downloaded from the Internet. It's also instructive to compare a sequence of surrealist-based images, such as the ones we used, with more realistic works. Counterintuitively, I'd suggest writing about the surreal first as a step toward writing more perceptively about the realistic.

Lesson 29: Writing in a Museum/Writing about Architecture

An "engaged worldview" ought to give us the tools to go nearly anywhere and make personal, meaningful connections. One need not write a poem to make such connections. But there are all sorts of playful "moves" that poetry teaches us that can guide and enhance our attention to *anything*, including paintings. This is what happened on a day when fourteen of the students, along with Jill and I, rode the bus to the Columbus Museum of Art to write poems about the work they found.

Today, after the briefest of introductions, I sent them off to scatter around the museum, seeking the places and pieces they most wanted to write about. Then we would gather back at lunch to share what we'd found. They'd been writing poetry for over a month now . . . and I wanted to see what they could do on their own. With so much freedom and lack of specific models, the day became a kind of impromptu "test" of their skills—in observation as well as writing.

Consider one student's response. Nate was a thoughtful student who has the goal of being a lawyer one day. Note the kind of playful making of meaning he's done by projecting another world inside Mel Chin's "Spirit," a huge barrel suspended on a rope of prairie grass, filling a whole room:

> I sleep, I dream
> As most men do
> But I see things, visions
> This mammoth barrel, it's filled you see
> Filled with the hopes and wants of all kinds of
> People, men, women, children
> All of their most secret wants are stored here
> And I can see them
> I can see them as vividly as the sky on a clear day
> Sort of frightening when you consider it
> We all want the same thing
> Peace
> We just have different views on how to
> Get there
> Now you must understand this

For true peace will never be achieved
Until all of these opinions stored in this barrel
Are respected
My friends,
That is when we reach the peace
Not from wars, but from finding a perfect equilibrium
And living in harmony

Nate does not so much describe the work as leap off from it into ideas of his own. That was pretty common this day. When such leaps happened, and when the poem worked, the source was usually this: the student had "stood in the midst of the work" and made a personal connection, letting *something* of the physical presence of the painting or sculpture into their poems. That is no small achievement in itself—and comes close to establishing a more engaged worldview, but it suggests more work with writing from visual imagery would have helped them see even a bit more rather than that vague "something."

Jill herself gives us the best model for the kind of close-reading of a painting I'm talking about, something that does more to get inside the substance of color and conflict, angle and mood than the paint conveys. Notice how she doesn't shy away from the subject matter, or simplify it—a painting from 1940 of the union battles by Paul Cadmus called "Herrin Massacre." Jill calls it,

I Pull My Red Dress Up

Red fist upraised, a crimson pipe
A flame of orange hair, now drenched in sweat
A pitchfork's fang marks in pale flank, white shirt,
the bleeding eyes
A cross of faded roses by a naked knee
Red splattered tombstone framed in lilies, white

Looking on, hands stuffed in rusty pockets
Cigar emerging from the lurid cavern
of his mouth, he smiles
Another dribbles beer down his red sleeveless tee

Behind, where one man washed in blood lies silent
underneath a hanging tree
That woman hikes her red dress up
Checks out her stockings
Rests her foot upon the corpse, & laughs

—Jill Grubb, teacher

I include this here not just to show how attention to detail can make a poem nearly painterly, but also to indicate the skills these students' teacher brought to our task this day—and to all our time together. It could well be that sophomores in high school are not quite able to stay this close to the work at hand, though I don't know for sure. I do know Jill's ability to pay close attention to a painting is the model I would teach from, if I could find the way.

Finally, let's take a look at two poems by Sarah K. She was one who was able to take full advantage of the day and lift her perceiving and writing to a new level. She'd worked with grounding her words in specifics, played with metaphor enough to know what it could do when bent one way or another, and she'd tinkered with playful means of surrealism enough to know she wasn't stuck with only one way of seeing. Most of all, she had that inner drive to make substantial meaning out of her exchange with the paintings to which she put her sight.

Here's what she came up with when she considered the museum's tiny Georgia O'Keeffe, "Autumn Leaves," done at Lake George in the 1920s (see Figure 9.5). Consider the *stance* she's taken even before she touches her first word to the paper:

Leaves (Georgia O'Keeffe)

I am hidden
behind bold colors.

Mindlessly forgotten
darkenly concealed.

Constantly being judged
posing in darkness.

For I am the foundation
of the one you admire.

This is a poem, small as it is, one could hold in one's hand for quite a while, picking it up over and over again to admire the hidden values behind the carefully chosen words. It's a small painting, after all, and one with a lot of depth behind its deceptively colorful surface. Sarah chooses therefore to play with those depths, to be that voice of the "mindlessly forgotten."

As I've hinted elsewhere, writing poems about paintings is not easy. So much is already being done in the visual format that students (and adults) often jump over into pure abstraction, forgetting to ground their images in the material world. Without making too big a claim, I

Figure 9.5. Georgia O'Keeffe, "Autumn Leaves—Lake George"

think Sarah bridged the gap best between these two sides in her last poem of that morning, a take on George Bellows's painting, "Polo at Lakewood" (see Figure 9.6). Somehow in this piece she's found, if only for an instant, the mix of play and personality, scene and finesse, metaphor and physicality she'd been hovering around all the time. It's a poem of a moment, just as Bellows's painting is, yet it slides out of that frozen frame into something of an eternal realm; all without seeming to try.

Figure 9.6. George Bellows, "Polo at Lakewood"

George Bellows, "Polo at Lakewood"

Holding back, then letting go,
Constant movement.

Flaring horses chasing
What is unknown to them.

That doesn't matter,
Keep moving.

Eyes are gazing
Watching, never stopping.

Forward movement,
Riders leaning at the ground.

There, something is moving
It seems to be running.

Maybe that's because
I am chasing it.

Whew, that's a ride. Like her poem on the O'Keeffe, I could live inside this poem for quite some time, for the ending returns to the beginning—and the game goes on. What seems to be working here so well? For one, it's the control of her lines. She's aptly chosen a two-line stanza; one quite suited to the quick movement of her subject. Each grouping then forms a unit of its own, establishing placement and then guiding us forward. It's a kind of a generic opening, not making clear who is speaking, yet that jarring lets us into the scene, as if we've been plunked smack in the middle of the game: "Holding back, then letting go / Constant movement."

The second stanza holds another mystery all its own, giving us a mix of sudden physicality ("flaring horses") followed by the metaphorical mystery of how they could be chasing "what is unknown to them." Then we are into some other point of view—and we guess there is a *presence* speaking these words: "That doesn't matter / Keep moving." An inner drive perhaps, inside one of the riders?

We get an "outside view" now in that wonderfully physical line: "Riders leaning at the ground." At the ground! Ah, Sarah, I want to say, you've found a way at last of putting us inside the horseman's view. And I'm hooked. Yes—the ball is alive. It has a life of its own, traveling the ground like a low-flying bird, with more momentum than we'd suspect from the last whack. *There*. The word takes on immense power, placed as it is in this context of motion, for "there" in this case is not specifically anywhere, just as the ball is a hazy presence within Bellows's canvas. The poem pulls to a close now, but it carries us onward, aware that pursuit is the whole of the game.

Coda: Poems about Architecture

Intriguingly, some of the best poems written this day came from our last exhibit: some architectural models of recent museums built around the world from a traveling exhibition, "Museums for a New Millennium." We received a wonderful tour from Dr. Tony Scott, then director of school programs at the museum, who used his extensive training in architecture to draw us into the process one goes through in designing a building. Soft-spoken and academic, Tony nevertheless held the kids spellbound as he told what he called the story of museum architecture, revealing the stunning features of each site—and the architect's choices hidden in each structure.

After the tour, I suggested that the students think of the museum as "the artist's house," and used as my model the title of Milkweed Editions's wonderful anthology of contemporary poems about visual art aptly titled *The Poet Dreaming in the Artist's House*, suggesting this basic way to respond:

> Describe the building in poem form using the phrase, "The artist's house is . . . "
> "The artist's house has . . . "
> "The artist's house is like . . . "

Act like it is alive, for it *is* alive with the architect's dream. In your poem, imagine being a part of that dream, as if you could climb up inside it.

What struck me most about their poems was: (1) how personal they are, and how much they made their own connections with the buildings; and (2) how vulnerable they became in the face of the architecture, as if the museums evoked some response in them that made them feel a part of the space, which is what I suppose the architects were after all along.

David C., for example, chose one of the more boxy, glass-enclosed shapes: *Cartier Foundation for Contemporary Art (France)—Jean Nouel, architect.*

> You seem microscopic compared to other great buildings
> but to me you are the grandest of all.
> You're open, transparent to the rest of the world.
> A view from your stair is amazing, different, free.
> I shouldn't feel hidden in you, but I do.
> I like it though.
> For inside you I am lost in myself.
> Others can't find me.
> Stay.

David here is responding to Tony's story about the Cartier Foundation building standing out so dramatically from the more traditional, Doric-column buildings that surround it. With nothing but its glass front, it says something quite different, using a paradoxical open-hiddenness, an effect that David has picked up on in his poem.

Bethany's poem seems equally "in-volved," held inside the structure as if in a fully constructed building. Is that the value of models like these, that even more than the actual structures, they allow us to project ourselves into their full dimensions, in contrast to the completed work, where we might not be able to step outside each individual section? A building *holds us*, in ways we often forget, the way her poem does:

> **The Tate**
>
> If I would look out
> the window I would see
> endless space below me
>
> Stretching down, kissing the water
> Pondering up in the sky,
> Balancing, imagining
> I am falling
>
> Drawing my own picture
> Like a lighthouse or a soldier
> Keeping the night under your wing

> Caressing our eyes
> the brilliance and solidness
> keeps me comforted, kindly
>
> Will you let me down now?

Here Bethany has taken us inside the work, without elaborate description. Her praise of the Tate opens up the most positive aspects of the model. It is a hymn to the power of museums themselves.

That's what I felt the most, as we wandered and looked, listened and wrote, in this final space of the day. After spending the day looking at art, we had been given a chance to look at—or ponder—our own vision. The whole wonder of museums came back to me as places to dream, to escape, to enter. I couldn't help believing that these kids would be back. Some of them were beaming with a kind of joy I hadn't seen on their faces before; they were just plain happy to be here.

Once again, it was Kelley who took the assignment to its fullest potential. Viewing the only building designed by a female architect (which is also the least conventional building in the group), she layered her seeing with a mixture of direct observation and inventive dreaming. She calls it, appropriately, "The Artist's House."

> The artist's house is like the deep red
> coral you find only at the bottom
> of the sandy ocean.
> It was once nothing
> but a puddle of flames, forever burning higher.
> Sometimes the layers mold together
> like the rising lava of erupting volcanoes.
> Suppose you were that old piano
> tucked away in the darkened
> basement of its under tunnels . . .
> would you still play your rusty
> tunes or whimper in the shadows of
> the corner for fear you will
> rock its layers of brilliance into shattered nothings?
> You are like my distorted dreams,
> twisting things when I climb inside
> you. My memory fades
> and in my dream,
> you are the reality of my own
> twisted thoughts.
> You have power over me,
> breaking my already
> shallow memory.
> I feel like my eyes pop out
> and intertwine with your

crazed illusions.
I carry a china cup filled
with luscious grapes
climbing to the top.
I gracefully toss the precious china
as it eternally falls, and like me,
passes your extraordinary wonders, thinking nothing.

Yes, you'd still need to see this amazing building to apply what Kelley has done here, but notice how the physical presence of what she was writing about influences the poem itself, shaping her choice of imagery. What's even more amazing are the physical dimensions she tucks into each line: "my eyes pop out / and intertwine with your / crazed illusions." Even the opening image of "the deep red / coral you find only at the bottom / of the sandy ocean" that "was once nothing . . . / but a puddle of flames." Looking at the building, one can find that burning coral, for the poem is an organic fusion of tunnels and colors, distortions and presence, just like the building is. All of art seems to be falling with Kelley as she holds that cargo of precious grapes. This seems to me to be interpretation at work, interpretation in the form of a poem.

Applying the Lesson on Your Own

Museums, large and small, are often within an hour's drive of many schools. And what better place to test out some of the connections between the visual and verbal worlds we've been exploring? I often ask if tours are available— anything that can help the students get the lay of the land. With groups you can trust, it's fun to let them go back to three or so works they noticed on the tour and find their own ways to create poems from the paintings. Some guidelines are helpful, even for advanced groups, lest they get lost in "talking about," rather than "from" or "to" the paintings and other artwork. (See Lessons 1, 7, 14, and 28 for some other approaches.)

Lesson 30: Writing about Their Own Photographs

For our final assignment, I procured some cameras from local businesses and asked the students, on their own, to go out and take some pictures. I gave them some hints to begin with based on some example photographs from John Szwarki's evocative book, *Looking at Photographs.* I wanted them to search for angles beyond the "video-eye" one we have

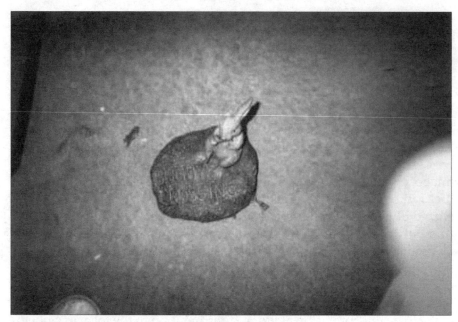

Figure 9.7. Amber, student, "Bunny Crossing"

all grown so used to, anything that might, like their poetry, shape a point of view. Slowly the photographs came in, and I have to admit, from the moment I saw them, I was mesmerized; partly because I'd never had a chance to give an art-making assignment before, but also because of the naive nature of their pictures, the touching rawness of them. As with the work of some "outsider" artists, even the mistakes, the awkward angles and blurs, suggested to me a poetic potential. These were *not* the photographs they would have taken on their own—not family snapshots or vacation scenes; not even exactly pretty. And yet they retained some of the "justness" of snapshot photography. They take on the ordinary life of these students—piano lessons, the stuff in their rooms, the barn slats, the stairs they walk down to breakfast every day, the bus ride past the horse corral—and, without trying to, create a kind of self-made ethnographic study of their world; warts and all. Let's look at three, each one flawed in some way.

Figure 9.7 is a photograph of one of the hundreds of little trinkets one might find in any craft or gift store anywhere across the United States. It is, I imagine, meant to be cute or whimsical—the sort of emotion highly privileged in such shops, one would guess, particularly by women (I cannot imagine a male over the age of ten thinking this item was worth purchasing or giving as a present). It may be produced to place in someone's backyard garden as a miniature token of the world of animals we have so successfully banished from our lives. It's not the item itself, then, that makes me laugh, but the angle from which Amber, the photographer, has chosen to view it; thumb intrusion and all, including part of the toe of her sneaker. From that "upper" vantage point, she asks us to see a clay model of a bunny propped upon its tiny world of a blue clay rock engraved with the words "Bunny Crossing" in orange block letters. From there I sense a grand distance between the viewers (us and the photographer) and that tiny world of this kind of artifact with which we so readily fill our contemporary homes. A meaningless object, really, and yet somehow worth giving to someone we love, maybe even "loved," if only for a short time in the recipient's life. It is treasured for that very whimsicality, or because it fits into a collection of "bunnies" the receiver is known to treasure. The world doesn't matter very much, this bunny says; the world of grades and stock portfolios, of college applications and army recruitment posters. It's the "little people" that do; the creatures not much paid attention to in the world of importance swirling all around us. This is Winnie the Pooh, Peter Rabbit, and Bambi resurrected in a gift item. If it is indeed Amber's possession, she's giving it to us now from the vantage point of a quickly maturing teen, one who some days—as she told me—takes the night off to gorge on chocolates and watch "chick flicks" and who decorates her wall with "hulk posters" of near-naked men. From *that* distance, she gives us Bunny Crossing, an out-of-focus photograph with her thumb intruding. A world she still owns but from which she is quickly separating.

Figure 9.8 is another small animal shot, this one with the subject alive. It intrigues, again, because of the view of the photographer, who has chosen to place the lens directly on the subject, but from a distorted under-angle so that the bird—a white or yellowish canary I believe—is caught within its tiny world. This is the picture of majesty tilted as if it has been poured into a frame. Nothing from the outside intrudes; no foot or thumb as in Amber's picture. Emma, a quiet, conscientious yet critically thinking student easily missed in the blur of much more demanding friends, has caught this portrait of herself, it seems, in the bird's black pupil nearly obscured by one bar of the cage.

What does it mean that yet a third photograph of an animal contained in a frame (Figure 9.9) attracts my eye? Maybe it's because the *body* has again inadvertently become the subject of the picture, or rather the angle of the photographer as she attempts to observe that body via

Figures 9.8 and 9.9. Emma, student, "Bird Cage" and Rachel, student, "Horse from a Bus Window"

the optic world of the camera. Here we have another off-angled shot; this one taken from a bus window. Rachel told me in passing that they watch the horse every day on their repetitive ride home. It's a high point in their routine, and she's done at least a little to bring out the animal's vibrant presence from within the dark world of the school bus, with its stiff and bulky vinyl seats. It seems significant that the metal crossbar of the bus window runs across the forehead of the horse, almost matching in size and color its restraining bridle. As with Emma's canary, the dark circle of what we know is the compelling eye of the mare is nearly eclipsed by the bar of the frame. In that framing something vital wants to emerge—into Rachel's knowing and into ours. And we view its presence from a nearly underwater world, from a half-chosen submersion—in the half-heard school talk, in everyday half-seeing, in the somewhat repressive and staunchly organized world of the school day—into a dreamt-of freedom. If Amber's toy rabbit photograph is saying goodbye, and Emma's bird is calling us in, Rachel's horse is greeting a world yet to be.

Intriguing as the students' photographs were, the poems that resulted were at first disappointing. Interviewing students afterwards confirmed my suspicions: they found it harder to write about these photographs because they knew the subjects so well. Often when they wrote they chose the pictures they themselves had taken, so of course they were less able to step out of the scene and be inventive. Where they made strong metaphorical meaning from the paintings at the museum, and playfully surreal images from the slides of Magritte and O'Keeffe, and where they constructed compelling physical worlds from the black-and-white photographs of local history, here they went almost entirely abstract.

A single example will stand for nearly everything written on this day. I have to say that without the title and the mention of books in the second line, I would have had almost no way of picking out this photograph (Figure 9.10) from the ninety-nine others laid out on the floor that day.

In between the Books

I'm hiding from the realm of society,
in between two books.
I'm still judged.

I see my faith or some of it.
It sees what I think is me.

But it doesn't see what is really me.
The walls and the people are no different.
Someone is caring for me for I cannot go it alone.

I don't know the way but it knows me
for it has seen me many times before.

If these walls could talk that's what they
are supposed to say but they won't say it.

All I know is the way.
I'm to the point where I don't care.

Coming from Ben V., who had written so insightfully before, his poem is especially disappointing. It's almost like his last line has bled all interest from the rest of the poem, or rather that the poem itself grows out of a deep lack of interest. I know from the exit interviews that Ben had gotten a lot out of the poetry this semester, so why this empty poem here at the end? If it were the only one, I'd chalk it up to his mood that day, but no, nearly every poem written was as flat as this.

Let's look at it briefly, perhaps to find hints as to why it's so weak. First of all, the scene is too loosely defined. Who is hiding? Where? If it's between the books, how are we supposed to picture that? As being squished? And why or how is he or it "still judged"? By whom? For what? Is the speaker a book himself? The whole poem is filled with "it" and "its" and "that's" (six instances); bland and passive verbs (seven instances of "is," "am"; four instances of the verb "to see,"), with the only other verbs being "hiding," "judged," "know," "say," and "care." All is kept so vague that we as readers are not made to care either.

Most of the students, like Ben, skipped past the photograph itself and went straight into some abstract world within the photograph, forgetting to *physicalize* their seeing, to *infuse metaphor*, to *play* with the actual relationships within the view. I should have had them list details, metaphors, and possibilities first, the way I had with the history photographs. Without such a brainstorming, the "strangeness that is our lives," so strong in my reading of these snapshots, could not come through.

Well, what to do? A solution didn't occur to me until my drive back the next morning, when muttering to myself I said, "They would have done better if they'd just written prose!" Aha—I thought. What if by going back to the pictures themselves and exploring them with prose this time, some new angle might emerge that might be added to the first draft? What resulted was our first successful effort in revision . . . and a good number of much stronger poems.

Here's an example, again by Ben V. It's not exactly a revision, as he started with a brand new photograph, but he seems to be tackling something of the same feelings. Only now he has found an inventive way of getting at those feelings through metaphor, inventive play, and attention to physical detail. He is writing about a photograph that I took of a wall outside the math room with algebraic figures painted around the doorway (Figure 9.11), a photograph where the shutter didn't fully open, so there are shadows closing in around the numbers.

> I see a blurp of math. A wall with writing about math. A wall that tells you how to do math. But some of it is absent. Like it felt

today. That part of the wall declined an interview. That part of
the wall didn't feel like watching again today without doing any-
thing about what it sees so it stayed home sick. Or maybe the
taker of the picture was hiding. Hiding somewhere in the big
shadows of two upper classmen, in between them, snapping a
shot of something it is not allowed to see like a paparazzi or me-
dia journalist. Seeing something it is not allowed to see. Some-
thing called knowledge. It goes to school because it has to. It wants
to learn, but it has to fit in. School doesn't teach it but school
impairs its learning ability.

Figures 9.10 and 9.11. Terry Hermsen, "Books" and "Math Wall"

What a stunning monologue to come from a flawed photograph! Here is the "I'm to the point where I don't care . . . " emotion of his poem from the previous day, but filled in with a "painted" scene and much fuller speculation. When I look again at the photograph he was writing from, I can actually *see* it from his point of view. Ben has put himself right there, in the photographer's place, and at the same time invented a little myth that digs into the whole nature of the school experience; a jaded myth, admittedly, but a compelling one.

What lessons can we glean from this day? Perhaps we'd come to rarify "the poem" too much. Perhaps photographs and other images supply *too* ready a way to construct a poem, without close attention to the details in the visual image first, so that the prose writing was a way for many of the students to really look. Certainly Heather's two writings would warrant such a claim. Here is what she wrote on the first day about a photograph of crisscrossing cloud patterns in a late evening sky (see Figure 9.12):

Figure 9.12. Student photographer, "Crisscross Clouds"

My eye is drawn
Past the delicate silhouette of the trees,
Past the obvious.
To the depths of never-ending sky.
Soft grays and blues,
Complementing the orange of a setting sun.
Cream clouds carefully painted
Crossing each other on the canvas of the cold sky
In brush strokes so thin,
So precise,
So vivid.

To whom shall I credit this masterpiece?

There was no kind way to tell Heather how bored I was by this poem. Admittedly, it's tough to write poems about sunsets without invoking the usual clichés, but just naming the colors and calling the sky a canvas does so little to capture the majesty we often feel when looking at such a sky, or in this case a photograph of such a sky. Yet look what she does when she just writes a straight series of observations about the photograph as such—what she likes about it and what it reminds her of:

I like how the clouds crisscross in the sky
It seems like a child's game
of tic-tac-toe
Suppose someone has sketched these lines
across the sky
I like how the setting sun looks golden
against the cold gray sky
It seems like there is chilled breeze
cutting through the trees
How did those clouds get there?
Suppose an airplane left them,
reminding all who gazed into the sky
that they too could fly.

What I like is how honestly Heather has expressed herself here, going straight to the photograph itself rather than to some code book of clichés of "how to look at a sunset." The tic-tac-toe reference is accurate—the first specific thing, besides generic colors, that she had written about the picture yet. And in the prose version even the colors get more precise: the golden sun against the cold gray sky. She speculates on a chilled breeze, which again makes *this* day at least somewhat more specific than the earlier version. And then she comes more touchingly to her question about authorship by simply asking, "How did those clouds get there?" She herself may have preferred the question of "To whom shall I credit this masterpiece?" But I have to respectfully disagree. As with many of the students on this second day of writing from their "photographs of now," the prose takes on its own seeing process and far outweighs the students' attempts to go straight to the poem.

One more example: this time, befittingly, from Shelby, writing—in prose—probably her best poem of the semester. On the first day with the photographs, like nearly everyone else, she'd forgotten to look carefully at all. And then something stunning happened. When I asked them to write prose this time—just noticing things and writing directly about what they saw—somewhere in the middle of the instructions I tossed out the possibility (off the top of my head) of "turning the photographs upside down." Only a few did, coming up with fresh results. Shelby went a step further—she turned the photograph (Figure 9.13) four different ways, writing what she thought were prose paragraphs about each one. And now, the student who had been one of the least inventive became one who could construct "little scenes" from even the most ordinary of pictures:

Blumpy Doughnuts

It looks like people are serving each other,
sharing the 'blumpness' of each doughnut,
everyone standing back waiting their turn.

It seems like someone is holding the pan side
ways, and will gradually let them slip to the ground.
The bakery has been attacked! (flipped/turned)

It may appear that the boys will soon be dumping
the doughnuts into a backpack and then making
a run for it.

They are trying to dump the doughnuts, they won't
fall off
The doughnuts seems to have a sweet glue that
keeps them bonded to the tray
Magnetic poles have strengthenly pulled
away from the boy and he uses his strength
to keep ahold

The sweet doughnuts glide down the raspberry
tray and land in the boy's hand
This, this is the chosen tray, hold thee above
all other doughnuts
A tasteful treat heading right to my mouth

Figure 9.13. Anonymous photographer, "Doughnuts"

Shelby was charged up by the end of this writing! She called me over, all excited, saying: "I think I finally got it!" Still, she claimed it wasn't a poem yet—until I showed her all the places she was doing exactly what a poem does—metaphorizing, inventing, describing, noticing small details, and imagining alternative possibilities. Frame by frame, as the photograph turns in her hands, she "explains" the new dimensions (and the defiance of gravity) in wildly logical ways. Now she can do what she could not do earlier: create, in a few words, a scene in her mind that responds to/interacts with the image in front of her.

Her language itself follows suit, becoming more risky and heightened when she needs it to. Again, as she did with "Mt. Gileadeans," she makes up new words when she has to: *blumpness* and *strengthenly*. And most magical of all, she borrows from her church experience to make the moment at the invaded bakery a "holy" moment (excuse the pun) with her line, "This is the chosen tray, hold thee above all other doughnuts."

This is a writer no longer afraid of failure, and one able to see and create and bask in the possibilities of her own creation. She is no longer worried about "what a poem is," and much more concerned with conveying her original vision. When she stood before the class that Friday afternoon and read her poem to us, she made quite an elaborate point of showing how each section was written from a different angle of the photograph. Others laughed, perhaps thinking she was going too far. I, on the other hand, was proud. Shelby had shown us all a new twist on how to see, and how to connect our words to enhance our relationship to even the most ordinary of aspects of the world around us. In a word, she was "engaged." And more than that, I think she knew it.

Applying the Lesson on Your Own

To end on a "less than successful" assignment, perhaps that's the first "lesson" here: to keep taking risks. Sometimes what we've planned or expected just doesn't turn out. So be it. That's the nature of art. It's the next step that counts—in this case, the chance to compare poetic versions with prose. Learning from our mistakes, I'd suggest reversing the process, asking the students to describe the photograph carefully in prose first, whether it's one of their own or a more professional one. Oh—and maybe that's the real lesson here: learning to look at their own photographs in something other than obvious ways.

Conclusion: Somewheres, Nowheres, and Elsewheres

In the end, maybe what matters most is what our students have to teach *us* about the nature of poetry. We can present them with all the materials, examples, and principles we can muster, but they will let us know, through their responses and their poems, what really gets through. Finishing a class with a group that's engaged, I often feel I've discovered the immense, intriguing, and open field of poetry all over again.

I believe poetry offers students one of the main resources to transform their lives, whether they live in troubled or sheltered, rural or urban, sophisticated or less privileged worlds. In all cases, the tools are nearly the same: learning how to look—how to see anything (including their own experience) with fresh eyes; learning to hear language as flexible material, full of metaphor and nuance, play and meaning; learning to visualize on the page, to make pictures happen, to construct *experiences* that are more than statements—that draw us to care; learning to take on other voices, to experiment with scenes-beyond-our-own; learning to dwell in moments, in textures, in tones, in as-close-to-the-physical as words can get; and learning to feel the words as they *turn* down the page, pulling us along. All this *can* be taught, to greater and lesser degrees, at their richest combination, providing a network of skills for students to rediscover who they are and where they are, and what matters to them.

Where they take it all is up to them, of course, as well as up to us as their teachers in terms of the assignments we provide. Can poetry be one of the forces working to resettle humanity, allowing us to hear each other and allowing us to reconnect with the places where we live? So this book contends. Many students' lives now seem so distant and disengaged, subsumed with cell phones, cars, video games, iPods, and malls. I want them to remember the richer sides of earth. The water that gives us life and that is so much in demand around the world. The streams and rivers all around us that we take for granted. The wind. The forest. The conversations of people on the street—people we *don't* know, rather than the few we text message or email. I want them to know that poetry can be a way of reconnecting with the past, while not being immune from the realities of the present. I want students to learn,

through poetry, to listen better to each other as well as to all that came
before us and all that will arise. I want them to *suppose* that language is
vibrant, that life is out there to be discovered, and that the pen and the
poem are vessels of wonder, ready to take them anywhere.

Where poetry took *us*, two years after "The Mt. Gilead Project,"
when these two classes of students were seniors, was a conference about
"Ethnography in Education" at the University of Pennsylvania in Phila-
delphia, where three students and Jill and I traveled by train to present
what we had done in terms of "global crises, local responses," the con-
ference theme for that year. The title of our presentation was rather
unwieldy, "Somewheres, Nowheres, and Elsewheres: Displacement and
Resettlement in an Age of Upheaval," but mainly we wanted to present
what we had done in the light of a world awash in migrations, exile,
and disconnection from place. What did our study in writing poetry over
the course of a semester in one town have to say about taking where
we are seriously—seriously enough to make it the source of poetry and
close study? Our consultant was Dr. Amy Shuman, director of the
Folklore Center at the Ohio State University, who brought up her coun-
seling of Somali refugees, hundreds of whom were trying to make a
"somewhere" out of Columbus, Ohio. Before presenting our work in
Mt. Gilead, I spoke also about the situation of the college where I now
teach, Otterbein, set in the once lily-white suburb of Westerville, whose
schools now contain students from many races and who represent sixty-
one different languages . . . and about my friend Christopher Merrill
who in his book, *The Old Bridge*, on the Bosnian War, refers to George
Steiner calling our times "the age of the refugee." Could we, I posited,
see these diverse trends as united, as part of a larger movement to re-
settle the earth, to make from undervalued "nowheres" or unchosen
"elsewheres" sustainable *somewheres* in which people might once again
feel a sense of pride and belonging?

For that bridge, I needed three other quotes. The first—an anony-
mous one—I found taped to the computer in my friend Colleen
Webster's house, where I'd stopped while en route to Philadelphia: "One
task of art is to articulate the missing links between the self and the
world. Another task—a higher task, I would say—is to forge new ones."
This is what we'd been doing during our Mt. Gilead Project, I suggested;
not just using writing to *record* our past responses to the town, but rather
drawing on the tools of art—all the ones we could muster—to form new
attachments, new associations, and new metaphors.

The second reference comes from ecologist David Orr's book *Earth
in Mind*. In that book he speaks of creating green cities, but also of the

need to make small, rural, and agrarian areas more livable. In our times, one of our deepest needs, he says, is to restore a sense of "home." As part of that process, he contends that "small towns must be revived and made inviting, viable, and accessible places. . . . I know of no formula for such a revival beyond pride and a love for one's community, plus *a dose of imagination for what it might be*" (197—emphasis mine). "For us," he continues, "coming home means restoring ecological and human scale to a civilization that has lost its sense of proportion and purpose" (202). Quite in parallel, though from a linguistic angle, my third quote came from Paul Ricouer, the prominent linguist, who says, "Imagination does not merely schematize the predictive assimilation between terms. . . . Rather, it contributes . . . to the projection of new possibilities of describing the world" (Sacks, 152).

New possibilities of describing the world. That's what these three students (Jordan, Greta, and Sarah) brought along, with Jill and me, as we began reading poems from their town, both their own poems and poems from others in their class. I'll allow them to have the last word. These poems come from an assignment done two years later in preparation for the trip, an exercise based in Georgia Heard's poem, "Where I Come From," but in which they do more than record little details of their present and past associations. Rather these young poets, as Ricouer and Colleen's anonymous philosopher would bid, *invent their way into the future.*

> I come from the chalky, alkaline dirt
> And air-pocketed mud of the Earth.
> But I must be from the ocean too,
> With miniscule creatures that rise up from
> And hum in my mind, or crash like
> Waves in my heart.
> How did I come from liquid life?
> Dark water in my songs.
> Dirt is my marrow, the boxer in my bones.
> My father says I hug the trees—he thinks that
> He does not.
> But oh he digs in the mud with me
> And plants the seeds that burst.
> He lived on a farm—the pigs ate his banjo.
> Does the crunch still sing in his ears?
> Where are <u>you</u> from, oh one who plowed
> The fields and played in mud?
> One who farmed the Earth?
> The snapping of the strings?
>
> —Mandy

I'm amazed by Mandy's ability here to work on many levels at once—the earthly and the watery, the universal and the particular. Clearly she's had something of an ongoing debate with her father about their mutual connections to the rural area they both claim as home, one that parallels our own national debate over the past century as we've migrated away from "the mud" and into paved towns and cities. What did he lose when the pigs ate his banjo (a real story, Mandy told us)? What will she create in her own songs, or in her own mud-pocketed, liquid life?

Josh, who wrote the next poem, read that day by his friend Jordan, is one of the few students in the school who had experienced a wide range of territories in his first eighteen years, spending his summers in Las Vegas and having lived in both Chicago and California for a spell. Star wrestler and center for the football team, Josh sports long blond hair and frequently wears chains on his low-hung baggy jeans. Yet he is as much an accepted and beloved member of his school as anyone, able to be brilliant in his studies yet maintain an edge of goofiness to his behavior. His poem here is direct and to the point:

> I come from a young mother and an irresponsible father
> I come from lust and was born a sort of semi burden
> I came as a blessing, a teacher of patience and virtue
> In the cramped apartment no one can escape
> She finds another and has another only this time no surprise
> Moving from Chicago to the sandy beaches and now to here
> Yet another man called dad
>
> —Josh

What to say? As in so many of Josh's poems, I'm *changed* after reading this. No riddle this time, he lets us know what all his moving and changes have meant. He makes us wonder what it must be like now to try to find "a home."

Three more poems, these from Jordan, Greta, and Sarah themselves, each one different in itself, yet combining to consider that same question of "where I come from."

> Chalk drawings on colored paper
> and an inherent love for music.
> I come from records and dance.
> The swimming grasses underwater
> like the raw dark smell of earth
> I come from twigs and language
> I come silent like a star—
> Ever-present and burning,
> singing stories in my mind about small things

with wings.
A great red chair that squeaks
and stones marking the lives of animal friends
I come from a sharp green air

—Greta

Can you feel the love and wonder in her lines? Caught in this moment of her late adolescence, Greta seems able to "see both ways;" back into childhood, "the small things with wings" that filled the fields around her, and also out into the "sharp green air" of adult awareness. No doubt this poem could be written anywhere, it seems so universal. But another part of me says: *No, this is Mt. Gilead. These are the "knowings" that have kept drawing me back to teach poetry there.*
As does Jordan's last poem:

I come from the woods
To see my grandfather
A sculptor of my life
Slowly shedding his self-indulgence
To show me what is truth

I come from the institution,
Where my mother told me
Hard, headlong orations of
How I can, and will.

I come from the kitchen
Where I smell her art,
Gramma's food,
That's where I found comfort in camaraderie

I go to a place
Without knowing the self sacrificing end
Illusions tell me it will be as hard as
The rock I was born from

I will be back

—Jordan

Jordan joined the Marines the next year—but still calls Jill from time to time to let her know how he is doing (last I heard, he was headed to Iraq). Whether he *will* return to Mt. Gilead in the future is another question. All I know is that he mentions to her how much our poetry time—and all his time in her class—has shaped how he sees the world. And I remember a moment midway in that semester of two years earlier, when Jill and I were somewhat "stuck" as to how to proceed. The classes had been going well, but something had stalled. We were only halfway through what we had wanted to cover, but we weren't sure the students were "with us." So we did what we hadn't thought of: we asked them.

Did they want to continue with the poetry? After some quite frank discussion, it was Jordan who turned the tide when he told us, "I really like this. No, it's not easy. And I can't say I always 'get' the poems. But they make me think." *They make me think.* I love that—and I will always remember that moment. And I hope that Jordan will apply, in his own way, all that we continued to explore.

Sarah K., too, took the occasion of the "I come from" assignment to ponder her future as well as her past—poised as she was, with the rest of her class, on the edge of graduation. She recently had traveled with her mother back to her family's roots in the Kentucky back country to attend her grandmother's funeral. She'd told me during our semester together that she spent much of her time, as she put it, "24/7 on the Internet," yet still treasured her long walk through tall pines down her driveway to the bus each morning, and her ability to whinny like a horse, as she showed us on that first day we started. In Kentucky, quite in contrast to her Internet-bound life, she experienced a world as it might have been a century ago—her grandmother's coffin laid out in the parlor, the whole family gathered around in mourning, singing the old songs through the night. She'd been shaken, she said, to see life so differently, and like Mandy, Josh, and Jordan, she'd come to weigh her life within a much larger frame, stretching back generations, even in these brief images:

A Beginning to a Past

calloused hands, pacing over
a few mellow strings
wired to a handmade mandolin
outside
chipped, painted panes
snow covered bean cages
gourds dangling shadows
silhouettes into the night

—Sarah K.

Looking back, perhaps this book as a whole forms a study of where these students "come from. . . ." It's dedicated to Jill Grubb and her three brave students (along with the thirty-nine others they represented) who took this journey with us. Perhaps our time together—and their growing-up time in Mt. Gilead—will remain mostly a way station in their passage out into a rapidly changing world. Or perhaps it could foreshadow a part of the larger picture ecologist David Orr holds out in *Earth in Mind*: a process of coming to dwell in more of a chosen place, a known place, a place of the heart they can return to, a *somewhere*, even as they also move out to worlds beyond.

Works Cited

Adair, Virginia Hamilton. *Ants on the Melon: A Collection of Poems*. New York: Modern Library, 1999.

Anderson, Maggie. *Years That Answer*. New York: Harper & Row, 1980.

Arnheim, Rudolf. *Visual Thinking*. Berkeley: University of California Press, 1969.

Arnow, Harriette. *The Dollmaker*. New York: Macmillan, 1954.

Bal, Mieke. *On Meaning-Making: Essays in Semiotics*. Sonoma, CA: Polebridge Press, 1994.

Bal, Mieke. *Reading "Rembrandt": Beyond the Word-Image Opposition*. Cambridge: Cambridge University Press, 1991.

Barfield, Owen. *Poetic Diction: A Study in Meaning*. Middletown, CT: Wesleyan University Press, 1973.

Bateson, Gregory. *Steps to an Ecology of Mind*. New York: Ballantine Books, 1972.

Behn, Robin, and Chase Twitchell. *The Practice of Poetry: Writing Exercises from Poets Who Teach*. New York: HarperPerennial, 1992.

Berger, John. *About Looking*. New York: Pantheon Books, 1980.

Berman, Morris. *The Reenchantment of the World*. Ithaca: Cornell University Press, 1981.

Brown, Kurt. *Verse and Universe: Poems about Science and Mathematics*. Minneapolis: Milkweed Editions, 1998.

Bruegel, Pieter, and Wolfgang Stechow. *Pieter Bruegel the Elder*. New York: H. N. Abrams, 1990.

Cacciari, Cristina, Maria Chiara Levorato, and Piercarla Cicogna. "Imagination at Work: Conceptual and Linguistic Creativity in Children." *Creative Thought: An Investigation of Conceptual Structures and Processes*. Eds. Thomas Ward, Steven Smith, and Jyotsna Vaid. Washington, D.C.: American Psychological Association, 1997.

Ciardi, John, and Miller Williams. *How Does a Poem Mean?* Boston: Houghton, Mifflin, 1975.

Cobb, Edith. *The Ecology of Imagination in Childhood*. New York: Columbia University Press, 1977.

Coleridge, Samuel Taylor. "Biographia Literaria" (sel.). *The Norton Anthology of English Literature*. Vol. 2. Ed. M. H. Abrams et al. New York: Norton, 1968.

Collins, Jeff, Howard Selina, and Richard Appignanesi. *Introducing Heidegger*. New York: Totem Books, 1999.

Dunn, Stephen. "Bringing the Strange Home." *Walking Light: Memoirs and Essays on Poetry*. Rochester, NY: BOA Editions, 2001.

Evans, David Allen. "Pole Vaulter." *This Sporting Life*. Eds. Emilie Buchwald and Ruth Roston. Minneapolis: Milkweed Editions, 1987.

Frost, Robert. *Selected Prose of Robert Frost*. Eds. H. Cox and E. Lathem. New York: Collier Books, 1966.

Frost, Robert. *The Poetry of Robert Frost*. Ed. E. Lathem. New York: Holt, Rinehart, and Winston, 1969.

Gadamer, Hans-Georg. *Heidegger's Ways*. Albany: State University of New York Press, 1994.

Gadamer, Hans-Georg, and Robert Bernasconi. *The Relevance of the Beautiful*. Cambridge: Cambridge University Press, 1986.

Ghiselin, Brewster. "Foreword." *Modern Poetry of Western America*. Eds. Clinton F. Larson and William Stafford. Provo, UT: Brigham Young University Press, 1975.

Gundy, Jeff. *Inquiries: Poems*. Huron, Ohio: Bottom Dog Press, 1992.

Hall, Donald. *Goatfoot Milktongue Twinbird*. Ann Arbor: University of Michigan Press, 1978.

Hass, Robert. "Basho Matsuo, Buson Yosa, and Issa Kobayashi." *The Essential Haiku: Versions of Basho, Buson, and Issa*. Hopewell, NJ: Ecco Press, 1994.

Hawkes, Terence. *Structuralism and Semiotics*. Berkeley: University of California Press, 1977.

Heidegger, Martin. "The Origins of the Work of Art." *Poetry, Language, Thought*. New York: Harper & Row, 1971.

Hermsen, Terry. "How to Do a Poetry Night Hike." *Teaching Writing from a Writer's Point of View*. Eds. Terry Hermsen and Robert Fox. Urbana, IL: National Council of Teachers of English, 1998.

Hermsen, Terry. "Kid-Talk/Art-Talk: Learning to Listen to the Kids We Teach." *Teaching Artist Journal* 3.1 (2005).

Hermsen, Terry. *The River's Daughter*. Huron, Ohio: Bottom Dog Press, 2008.

Hermsen, Terry, and Robert Fox. *Teaching Writing from a Writer's Point of View*. Urbana, IL: National Council of Teachers of English, 1998.

Hilberry, Conrad. *The Moon Seen as a Slice of Pineapple*. Athens: University of Georgia Press, 1984.

Huizinga, Johan. *Homo Ludens: A Study in the Play-Element in Culture*. London: Routledge & Kegan Paul, 1949.

Jakobson, Roman. "What Is Poetry?" *Semiotics of Art: Prague School Contributions*. Eds. Ladislav Matejka and I. R. Titunuk. Cambridge, MA: MIT Press, 1976. pp.164–175.

Jephcott, E. F. N. *Proust and Rilke: The Literature of Expanded Consciousness*. New York: Barnes and Noble Books, 1972.

Jiménez, Juan Ramón. "Oceans." *News of the Universe: Poems of Twofold Consciousness*. Ed. Robert Bly. San Francisco: Sierra Club Books, 1980.

Johnson, Mark. *The Body in the Mind: The Bodily Basis of Meaning, Imagination, and Reason*. Chicago: University of Chicago Press, 1987.

Karpowicz, Tymoteusz. "The Pencil's Dream." *Postwar Polish Poetry: An Anthology*. Ed. Czeslaw Milosz. Berkeley: University of California Press, 1983.

Lakoff, George, and Mark Turner. *More Than Cool Reason: A Field Guide to Poetic Metaphor*. Chicago: University of Chicago Press, 1989.

Lee, Harper. *To Kill a Mockingbird*. New York: Warner Books, 1960.

Leslau, Charlotte, Wolf Leslau, and Jeff Hill. *African Proverbs*. New York: Peter Pauper Press, 1985.

Levertov, Denise. *The Jacob's Ladder: Poems*. New York: A New Directions Paperbook, 1961.

Lorca, Federico García. *Canciones*. Granada: Comares DL, 1998.

Matthews, J. H. *The Surrealist Mind*. Selinsgrove, PA: Susquehanna University Press, 1991.

Mearns, Hughes. *Creative Power: The Education of Youth in the Creative Arts*. New York: Dover Editions, 1929.

Merrill, Christopher, and David St. John. *Watch Fire: Poems*. Fredonia, NY: White Pine Press, 1994.

Merwin, W. S. *East Window: The Asian Translations*. Port Townsend, WA: Copper Canyon Press, 1999.

Miller, Arthur. *The Crucible: A Play in Four Acts*. New York: Bantam Books, 1959.

Mitchell, W. J. Thomas. *Iconology: Image, Text, Ideology*. Chicago: University of Chicago Press, 1986.

Mitchell, W. J. Thomas. *Picture Theory: Essays on Verbal and Visual Representation*. Chicago: University of Chicago Press, 1994.

Nabhan, Gary Paul, and Stephen Trimble. *The Geography of Childhood: Why Children Need Wild Places*. Boston: Beacon Press, 1994.

Nemerov, Howard. *The Blue Swallows: Poems*. Chicago: University of Chicago Press, 1969.

Neruda, Pablo. *Memoirs*. New York: Farrar, Straus & Giroux, 1977.

Neruda, Pablo. *Toward the Splendid City: Nobel Lecture*. New York: Farrar, Straus & Giroux, 1972.

O'Hara, Frank, and Donald Merriam Allen. *The Collected Poems of Frank O'Hara*. Berkeley: University of California Press, 1995.

Oresick, Peter, and Nicholas Coles. *Working Classics: Poems on Industrial Life*. Urbana: University of Illinois Press, 1990.

Orr, David W. *Earth in Mind: On Education, Environment, and the Human Prospect.* Washington, DC: Island Press, 1994.

Orr, Gregory. *Gathering the Bones Together: Poems.* New York: Harper & Row, 1975.

Ozick, Cynthia. *Metaphor and Memory: Essays.* New York: Vintage Books, 1991.

Poirier, Richard. *Robert Frost: The Work of Knowing.* New York: Oxford University Press, 1977.

Raab, Lawrence. *Mysteries of the Horizon.* New York: Doubleday, 1972.

Ricoeur, Paul. "The Metaphorical Process as Cognition, Imagination, and Feeli≤/." *On Metaphor.* Ed. Sheldon Sacks. Chicago: University of Chicago Press, 1978.

Rilke, Rainer Maria, and Robert Bly. *The Selected Poems of Rainer Maria Rilke.* New York: Harper & Row, 1981.

Rogers, Pattiann. *Firekeeper: New & Selected Poems.* Minneapolis: Milkweed Editions, 1994.

Rothenberg, Jerome, "Bantu Combinations" in *Technicians of the Sacred: A Range of Poetries from Africa, America, Asia & Oceania.* New York: Anchor Books, 1969.

Sandburg, Carl. *Complete Poems.* New York: Harcourt Brace, 1950.

Scott, Nathan A. "Coleridge on the Dignity of the Poetic Imagination" and "Heidegger's Vision of Poetry as Ontology." *The Poetics of Belief: Studies in Coleridge, Arnold, Pater, Santayana, Stevens, and Heidegger.* Chapel Hill: University of North Carolina Press, 1985.

Shinder, Jason. *Lights, Camera, Poetry!: American Movie Poems the First Hundred Years.* San Diego: Harcourt Brace, 1996.

Simic, Charles. *Selected Early Poems.* New York: George Braziller, 1999.

Singer, Jerome L. "Imaginative Play in Childhood: Precursor of Subjective Thoughts, Daydreaming, and Adult Pretending Games." *The Future of Play Theory: A Multidisciplinary Inquiry into the Contributions of Brian Sutton-Smith.* Eds. Brian Sutton-Smith and Anthony D. Pellegrini. Albany: State University of New York Press, 1995.

Snyder, Gary. *Riprap, & Cold Mountain Poems.* San Francisco: Four Seasons Foundation, 1969.

Sontag, Susan. *On Photography.* New York: Dell Pub. Co., 1977.

Stafford, William. *Allegiances.* New York: Harper & Row, 1970.

Stanford, Ann. *The Weathercock.* San Jose: Talisman Press, 1956.

Stewart, Susan. *Nonsense: Aspects of Intertextuality in Folklore and Literature.* Baltimore: Johns Hopkins University Press, 1979.

Sutton-Smith, Brian. "A 'Sportive' Theory of Play." *Play and Culture.* Ed. Helen B. Schwartzman. West Point, NY: Leisure Press, 1980.

Szarkowski, John. *Looking at Photographs: 100 Pictures from the Collection of the Museum of Modern Art.* New York: The Museum of Modern Art, 1973.

Szymborska, Wislawa, Stanislaw Baranczak, and Clare Cavanagh. *View With a Grain of Sand: Selected Poems.* New York: Harcourt Brace and Co., 1995.

Thrall, William Flint, and Addison Hibbard. *A Handbook to Literature.* New York: The Odyssey Press, 1960.

Walker, Sydney R. *Teaching Meaning in Artmaking.* Worcester, MA: Davis Publications, 2001.

Welsh, Andrew. *Roots of Lyric: Primitive Poetry and Modern Poetics.* Princeton: Princeton University Press, 1978.

Wheelwright, Philip Ellis. *Metaphor & Reality.* Bloomington: Indiana University Press, 1962.

Williams, William Carlos, and Charles Tomlinson. *Selected Poems.* New York: New Directions, 1985.

Wright, James Arlington. *The Branch Will Not Break: Poems.* Middletown, CT: Wesleyan University Press, 1963.

Yeats, W. B., and M. L. Rosenthal. *Selected Poems.* New York: Macmillan, 1962.

Index

Author

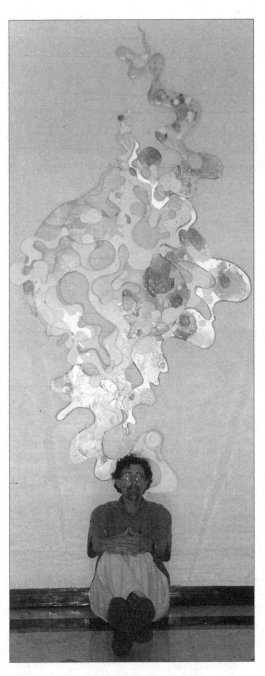

Terry Hermsen has lived in Ohio since 1972. He has a BA in English from Wittenberg University, an MFA in poetry from Goddard College, and a PhD in art education from The Ohio State University, and teaches poetry, composition, and literature at Otterbein College. From 1979 to 2004, he taught poetry all around the state via the Ohio Arts Council's Artists in Education program, teaching students from kindergarten through high school, as well as senior citizens and other adults. For five summers he was on the faculty of the Antioch Writers Workshop; and he taught in the first five years of the Ohio Arts Council's Experience of Writing summer workshops for teachers, coediting (with Bob Fox) the anthology that grew out of those years, *Teaching Writing from a Writer's Point of View.* Additionally, he was on the faculty of the OAC's Summer Media Institute from 1998–2003. He has taught poetry in the galleries of various museums throughout the state, including the Allen Art Museum in Oberlin, the Toledo Museum of Art, and the Cleveland Museum of Art; and for seven years he was a guest poet with the Columbus Museum of Art's DepARTures program, guiding fifth graders from around the city on poetry-writing tours of the museum. His most recent book of poems is *The River's Daughter* (2008) from Bottom Dog Press.

෬

This book was typeset in Palatino and Helvetica by Electronic Imaging.
Typeface used on the cover were Stanyan, Rockwell, and Torino.
The book was printed on 50-lb. Williamsburg Offset paper by Versa Press, Inc.